ANDREW MURRAY
THE AUTHORIZED BIOGRAPHY

ANDREW MURRAY
THE AUTHORIZED BIOGRAPHY

Leona Choy
FOREWORD BY REV. BARRY MURRAY

Fort Washington, PA 19034

Andrew Murray: The Authorized Biography
Published by CLC Publications

U.S.A.
P.O. Box 1449, Fort Washington, PA 19034

UNITED KINGDOM
CLC International (UK)
Unit 5, Glendale Avenue, Sandycroft, Flintshire, CH5 2QP

© 2000 Leona Choy
All rights reserved. Published 2004
This printing 2017

Printed in the United States of America

ISBN (paperback): 978-0-87508-829-7
ISBN (e-book): 978-1-61958-105-0

Unless otherwise noted, scripture quotations marked NASB are from the New American Standard Bible® (NASB), Copyright © 1960, 1962, 1963, 1968, 1971, 1972, 1973, 1975, 1977, 1995 by The Lockman Foundation. Used by permission. www.Lockman.org

The Murray family and the Andrew Murray Family Association of South Africa, insofar as it is their right to do so, have granted the author their necessary permission to use the information they have provided for her book, with the understanding that appropriate acknowledgment will always go with the use of the information and that the copyright or other rights pertaining to the information or to the family and/or the Association will not in any way whatsoever be jeopardized, impeded or negatively affected thereby.

About the Author

Born of Czech parents in Iowa and a graduate of Wheaton College, Illinois, Leona Choy served with her late husband, Ted, in mission, church and educational work in Hong Kong, Singapore, China and the United States. Co-founder of Ambassadors For Christ, Inc., a campus ministry among Chinese university students and scholars, her quarter century of work was administrative and editorial.

Fourteen trips to the People's Republic of China as guide/escort and English teaching consultant enriched her research and experiences for writing. As President of WTRM-FM (Southern Light Gospel Music Network) in the Shenandoah Valley of Virginia, Leona produced a daily radio program for five years.

Leona is the author, editor or collaborator of over thirty published books and twelve foreign language editions; her articles have appeared in over seventy different periodicals. Her poems have been published in scores of magazines and read over her daily radio programs *Intensive Care* and *Living It Up* on WTRM.

She is managing editor of Golden Morning Publishing in Winchester, Virginia, where she makes her home. Four grown sons, ten grandchildren and a great grandchild keep her busy when she isn't writing or traveling.

Contents

Foreword • 9
Preface • 11
Acknowledgments • 15
Portrait by Pen • 17
Introduction — Here Was a Man • 21

Chapter 1	Deep Roots for Strong Trees • 25	
Chapter 2	Sturdy Branches Spread • 35	
Chapter 3	The Chocolate Club • 41	
Chapter 4	God's Wilderness Classroom • 49	
Chapter 5	Vacations for Spiritual Trek • 55	
Chapter 6	A Bride Prepared • 59	
Chapter 7	Covered Wagon Honeymoon • 71	
Chapter 8	"A New Idea of a Wife" • 77	
Chapter 9	The Nest God Intended • 85	
Chapter 10	Revival at Last • 95	
Chapter 11	Fruit that Remains • 105	
Chapter 12	Urban Parish and Court Battles • 109	
Chapter 13	Pastorate in a Pasture • 115	
Chapter 14	Commit to Faithful Persons • 125	
Chapter 15	"Quite a Lion" in America • 133	
Chapter 16	Revival Winds Blow South • 139	

Chapter 17	Made Perfect in Weakness • 143
	Photographs • 151
Chapter 18	The Afterward of Healing • 161
Chapter 19	Personal Testimony • 169
Chapter 20	Deeper Into Secrets • 179
Chapter 21	Missionary Statesman • 187
Chapter 22	Power for Outreach • 193
Chapter 23	An Anointed Pen • 201
Chapter 24	Ripening Years—Climbing Higher • 213
Chapter 25	The Family Touch • 225
Chapter 26	Not Sunset, But Promotion • 231
	Epilogue • 239

Register of the Children and Grandchildren • 245

Two Testimonies from South Africa • 247

Appendix of Murray Books • 249

Bibliography and Resources • 265

Other books by the author • 267

Foreword

On behalf of the Murray descendants in South Africa, and with the input of other family members, I consider it a privilege to be invited to write the Foreword to the expanded new edition of the biography of our respected ancestor, Dr. Andrew Murray.

The fact that his writings are still being read worldwide and continue to have an impact on thousands of lives even to this day is extraordinary. Likewise, Leona Choy's remarkable biography, *Andrew Murray: Apostle of Abiding Love*, was translated into many languages and continues to touch many lives here in South Africa and around the globe.

As did the original book, the additional chapters to the new edition make fascinating and blessed reading. Leona Choy was inspired by the Holy Spirit to bring a new focus on Emma, Andrew's God-given wife. Emma meant enormously much to Andrew as a person and as an intellectual and spiritual companion, and to his flocks as the minister's beloved, caring and devoted wife. She was spiritually outstanding, partly due to her upbringing by devoted parents in a Christian home and church environment, but above all as a result of the anointing of the Holy Spirit in her personal life. In any home, such a wife and mother is truly worth more than her weight in gold.

When the Reverend Andrew Murray Sr., father of Dr. Andrew Murray Jr., arrived in South Africa from Scotland and was ordained as minister of the Dutch Reformed Church in Graaff-Reinet in 1822, an unprecedented Murray ministry began. Eventually nine of Rev. Murray's eleven adult children and thirty-two of his grandchildren were directly or indirectly concerned with Christian ministry. Five of his six sons (including Andrew Jr., the subject of this book) became ministers, and four of his five daughters married ministers. As for the grandchildren, seventeen became ministers, twelve married ministers and three became missionaries.

Of the children of Andrew Jr. and Emma, three devoted their lives to full-time work in church and mission fields. Others served the Lord and their communities as teachers and in other careers.

Today the descendants of the Reverend Andrew Murray Sr. who live in South Africa number several thousand and run into eight generations. Of these, about a hundred are direct descendants of Andrew Jr. and Emma.

Through the generations, a relatively large proportion of the wider Graaff-Reinet Murray family continue to devote their lives to full-time or part-time ministry, notably in the mission fields of Africa and elsewhere. Others followed a wide spectrum of careers in different parts of the world, serving God's Kingdom and their fellow human beings.

All of us continue to be humbled, however, by the realization that being a member of this illustrious family is no qualification as such for entrance into the Kingdom of God. One's relationship with one's Maker and Savior remains a very personal matter.

As for the long and continuing chain of Murray descendants *even beyond* "children's children" who since 1822 entered and are still entering the service of our Lord Jesus Christ, we can only say: Praise the Lord!

Rev. Barry Murray (1998)
Honorary President: The Andrew Murray Family Association in South Africa

Preface

"It is wonderful how the written page can give back the spirit of a man with all its heroic influences."

The Andrew Murray of this story wrote the above words about *another* man's biography. If I am able by writing this book even to approach this high goal by providing new generations of readers with a living, human Andrew Murray, I am satisfied.

The books of this spiritual giant of yesterday have influenced my Christian life since my teens. A new believer at the time, I could barely understand their spiritual heights and depths in my immaturity, but I instinctively knew that this man of God beckoned me to start climbing a mountain that would take a lifetime to scale. Through my years of academic preparation, then ministry for the Lord on the mission field and in various avenues of Christian service, I read Murray's books over and over. I highlighted sentences which leaped into my spiritual horizon of need. I wrote dozens of poems sparked by phrases from his writings which spoke intensely to my spirit. Murray's soundly biblical teachings nourished and sustained me, drawing me to launch out into the deep with God.

But I always wanted to know more about *the man behind the words*. Was he real? Was he of like passions? What happened in his life to cause him to write with such deep conviction on certain themes? Did he have a sense of humor or was he always stern? Was he approachable? What was his family life like? Did he live on a pedestal or rub shoulders with ordinary people? Was he always strong in spiritual victory, or did he struggle and sometimes become discouraged like me?

A contemporary biography of Andrew Murray was long overdue. Early biographies were out-of-print and found only in library archives. There was a fullness of time for the first edition of this biography. I was commissioned by the publisher to write it to commemorate the 150th anniversary of Murray's birth in 1828.

I felt a keen sense of destiny, mingled with unworthiness, as if chosen by God (and with a smile and nod of approval from Andrew himself) to write a new biography. To research his life became a holy task. I experienced a spiritual high while digging into archives. I lived Murray's life vicariously to his last breath of praise when he finally beheld the Lord whom he loved and served with such fervor.

I alternately laughed and cried as I experienced tender and traumatic episodes of his life with him and Emma, his wife. I was spiritually enriched because I felt I knew him at last. I read his writings with this background of fresh understanding of the very human Andrew Murray. His teachings speak to my struggles in the flesh and to my triumphs in the Spirit. I call him "Andrew" throughout the book because I feel I know him from his boyhood. I think of him in the present tense and talk about him with my friends in that way. I expect to recognize him immediately some day in Glory when I meet him as part of the "communion of saints" from all ages. I hope you'll feel the same as you read this book.

This new edition commemorates the 173rd anniversary year of his birth. As I did for my original biography, *Andrew Murray: Apostle of Abiding Love*, published by Christian Literature Crusade, I sought and found additional information from sources in South Africa where the many descendants of Andrew Sr. (his father) and Andrew Jr. (as his descendants told me they differentiate them) still live, work, and serve the Lord in various capacities.

I drew especially upon two books available only from South Africa, both written by a granddaughter of the Murrays. She compiled the journals and family letters written by Emma giving us intimate material about her growing years in mid-Victorian Cape Town in the 1850s. They provide interesting insights about their courtship, marriage and family life. I added several new chapters to this edition so we may become better acquainted with Emma and understand the important role she played in Andrew's life for nearly fifty years.

In the Appendix I provide a synopsis of most of Murray's books in print, the date of their writing, and valuable cross references to the chapters in this book which give the setting and background of their writing.

The first edition of this biography was translated into Spanish, Dutch, Chinese, Afrikaans and Korean. As this book goes to press, it is being translated into Russian in the Ukraine. During my travels in The People's Republic of China, I met a Chinese woman in a small village who, when she heard my name, ran to her home and returned with a Chinese translation of my Murray biography. The pages were tattered, and the cover was partly missing from being passed around and read by nearly every Christian in the village. She hugged me tearfully and told me with joy how the farmer-pastor of the house church preached from it. After more than a century and a half, Andrew Murray's written words were still leading Chinese believers and the Christians of other nations into the deeper life in Christ.

Leona Choy (2000)

Acknowledgments and Dedication

I thank God for the opportunity, privileges and enabling to write this book. All glory to Him. I appreciate the help of the Murray family in South Africa and other friends there who so willingly provided valuable resources, archival photos, accurate information about Murray descendants, and affirmation and encouragement for this new edition. I dedicate this book to the descendants of Andrew Murray Sr., Andrew Jr. (the subject of this book) and Emma, his wife. They have received a godly heritage.

Special thanks to Rev. Barry Murray of Pretoria, honorary president of the Andrew Murray Family Association in South Africa and direct descendant of Andrew Murray, who wrote the Foreword. Also to Mr. Teo Louw, committee member and treasurer of the aforementioned Association, also a Murray descendant, who wrote the Epilogue.

Contacted and consulted for comments, support and relevant input were Betty Hirzel of Durban, her sister Peggy Corbett of Cape Town, and their cousins, the sisters Prudence Hobson and Wendy Kroon of Graaff-Reinet. All four are great-granddaughters of Andrew and Emma, and granddaughters of Andrew Haldane Murray. Also consulted were Emma Horn (Jemima branch) of Cape Town, an expert source of information on the family; Erika Murray-Theron (William branch) of Pretoria, an eminent local novelist in Afrikaans.

Helpful information was received from Rev. Albert Brandt of Stellenbosch, retired pastor of the Lutheran Church and doctoral candidate at the University of Stellenbosch in whose thesis Andrew Murray plays a major role; the Andrew Murray Centre and Wellington Museum and the South African Library in Cape Town. Thanks to Winnie Rust of Wellington for photos of Clairveaux and Felicity Grove of Stellenbosch for her e-mail assistance.

I acknowledge with thanks the following statement of permission from Teo Leow: "Insofar as it is in our rights to do so, we grant you on behalf of the Murray family and the Andrew Murray Family Association in South Africa, our necessary permission to use the information we have provided for your book, with the understanding that appropriate acknowledgment will always go with the use of the information and that the copyright or other rights pertaining to the information or to the family and/or the Association will not in any way whatsoever be jeopardized, impeded or negatively affected thereby."

Portrait By Pen

If you had an opportunity to meet Andrew Murray in person in the prime of his ministry, if you could shake his hand, have some private conversation with him, and then sit under his preaching as part of an audience numbering thousands, how would he impress you? How would you describe him physically? He was born and ministered before the invention of movies, videos or audio recording. We don't have the privilege of seeing Andrew Murray in action or hearing his voice. But we are given a treasured insight by the late Rev. H. V. Taylor which appeared in the *British Weekly* newspaper more than a hundred years ago, on December 6, 1894. The occasion was one of Andrew's visits to England, America, and Europe for conference ministry. Let us meet Andrew Murray through the eyes of a firsthand observer:

> The title of catholic . . . is most appropriate for this man of wide sympathies and love. "We are *Christian first* and Dutch Reformed afterward," he declared while addressing Synod delegates from many different churches of his denomination. This statement gives the keynote of his life.
>
> Mr. Murray desires to be known as a Christian, simply as a follower of Jesus. He seems to examine everyone he meets for the Christian element in him. This is the impression left on the mind when one is in conversation with him. His keen, yearning look scans the face of the one with whom he is speaking to see if the witness of the Christ-life is there, and to plead, above all things, for loyalty to his Master. You cannot help saying to yourself, "This man wants me to belong to Jesus Christ." No one who has talked with him, even on casual themes, can forget that wistful glance.

His nature is profoundly devotional; he carries with him the atmosphere of prayer. He seems always wrapped about with a mantle of adoration. When preaching or conducting a service, his whole being is thrown into the task and he glows with a fervency of spirit which it seems impossible for human flesh to sustain.

At times he startles and overwhelms listeners. Earnestness and power of the electric sort stream from him and affect the large audience in the same way as the quiet circle gathered around him.

In his slight, spent frame of middle height, he carries in repose a volcanic energy which, when he is roused, bursts its barriers and sweeps all before it. Then his form quivers and dilates, his lips tremble, his features work, his eyes spasmodically open and close, as from the white-hot furnace of his spirit he pours the molten torrent of his unstudied eloquence. The thin face and almost emaciated body are transfigured and illumined.

The staid, venerable minister of the nineteenth century, with the sober, clerical garb and stiff white tie, which is *de rigueur* among the Dutch clergy, disappears and an old Hebrew prophet stands before us—another Isaiah with his glowing imagery, a second Hosea with his plaintive, yearning appeals.

Audiences bend before the sweeping rain of his words like willows before a gale. The heart within the hearer is bowed, and the intellect awed. Andrew Murray's oratory is of that kind for which men willingly go into captivity.

His disposition is mystical. As in the best of mystics, the religious thought clothes a strong and fearless nature. No man can study his face without being struck by the inwardness of the deep-set grey eyes. Even when one gets to handgrips with him in closeness of company, one is conscious of the great part that remains unexpressed, the spiritual *hinterland* which extends far beyond the visible shore. There is always the suggestion of great strength held in reserve.

A student of character cannot help being convinced that if the old days of persecution were to return, *Andrew Murray would go to the stake as cheerfully as he steps up to the Moderator's chair!*

The Republic of South Africa issued a postage stamp in 1978 commemorating the 150th anniversary of the birth of Andrew Murray.

Here Was a Man

"Why hath the Lord put me in the ministry—unfit as I am—leaving me to wrestle with the awesome work in my own impotency? Oh! Why cannot I find the needful strength?" lamented young Andrew Murray Jr., fresh from seminary.

"HERE WAS A MAN, a discouraged minister barely twenty-five years old, struggling with his lack of spiritual power. Yet he was destined to become one of the best loved and most widely read writers on the deeper Christian life. In his eighty-eight years he wrote about 240 books and tracts which were published in fifteen languages. Many of his works are being eagerly reprinted today. He had an anointed pen because he had an anointed heart. He did eventually find that power from God for which he hungered, found it in "the full blessing of Pentecost," as he described it, in his personal life and ministry.

HERE WAS A MAN who since childhood heard his minister-father plead and pray with tears of anguish for revival, in which prayers Andrew joined. Yet he did not immediately recognize the outpouring of the Holy Spirit when it began to happen in his congregation. In fact, he sought to stop it until he was inundated with the Spirit himself, resulting in the transformation of his ministry.

HERE WAS A MAN who was famous too early, a boy preacher to whose meetings admiring crowds flocked, who could count conversions at every evangelistic service. He confessed to fighting the insidious inroads of pride as his archenemy. This was the man who wrote a masterpiece on humility after God dealt deeply with him.

HERE WAS A MAN most people know primarily for his devotional writings, but who was also a missionary force that shook his generation. A missionary statesman of whom churches and conventions took serious notice, he enlisted missionary candidates by the hundreds for pioneer works, giving his own sons and daughters for the missionary cause.

HERE WAS A MAN who was an educator, a founder of institutions for secular and religious training, who upgraded the academic standards of his country and times. He was involved on every level of community and national importance for the betterment of his fellow men.

HERE WAS A MAN—a church politician in the best sense of the word—who was a recognized leader from God in any gathering into which he stepped. Not all agreed with him, but his advice was sought and his wishes respected. His opinions counted with people of all ages and every degree of social standing. It was not because he was an authoritarian figure, but because he was known to be in constant touch with God. Six times elected Moderator of the Synod of the Dutch Reformed Church in South Africa, he defended the Faith in civil courts in his country and left a permanent mark on the denomination with which he served.

HERE WAS A MAN who worked for spiritual renewal within the established church and who reaped the results of his prayers and labors in a deep moving of the Holy Spirit not only in his parish, country, and generation, but even to the present day through his writings.

HERE WAS A MAN, a family man, a tender, loving husband and devoted father of eight children, who all his life had a special rapport with youngsters. He was always involved with youth, influencing young seminarians who lived in his home to develop godly characters and helping to shape their destinies. By no means always stern and serious, Murray was a man of laughter, humor and ready wit.

HERE WAS A MAN whose spirit ripened in maturing years to a full golden harvest in the setting sun, who lost no spiritual zest or optimism as his outer man grew more frail. He stepped over the final line separating our earthly now from eternity with an eager anticipation and genuine joy to see his God at last.

HERE WAS A MAN who was said to be "not a voice alone, but a force who created not merely an influence but an atmosphere for God." There were few in his country and generation who had not heard him preach or met him in person.

We, too, have an opportunity to MEET THIS MAN, Andrew Murray, in the pages that follow, and meet his wife, Emma. Andrew acknowledged that his books could never have been written without her.

First, let's meet Andrew as a winsome, fun-loving, young Scottish boy. . . .

1

Deep Roots for Strong Trees

"Good-bye! Good-bye, dear Mamma, Papa! See you soon!"

The lad of ten years, outfitted in an adult-styled, black suit with starched shirt and ruffled cuffs, held his stiff-brimmed hat on with one hand and waved frantically with the other. The wind whipped the words from his lips as the ship unfurled its sails and slipped away from the pier. He clung to the rail, swaying with the strange and uncomfortable ocean surge.

"Andrew, you shouldn't say *soon*. You know we will be away for a long, long time," corrected his brother, John. All of two inches taller and two years older, similarly clad in Sunday finery, the elder of the Murray brothers steadied himself and also continued to wave. Their voices could no longer be heard over the noise of the flapping sails and squeaks of the rings and rigging-ropes against the masts.

John saw large tears trickling down Andrew's pale face. The boy held them back bravely during the parting scene at Port Elizabeth, South Africa, where good-byes were exchanged with their father and mother and relatives. Now he could restrain them no longer. He sobbed quietly, biting his lip for control.

John put his arm awkwardly around the boy. "Andrew, God will always be with us just as He will be with Papa and Mamma. And with William, Maria, Charles and baby Jemima. Just think," he tried to divert Andrew's sadness with small talk, "Jemima might be as old as you are right now when we get back!"

Andrew giggled and stifled a sob at the same time in such a way that both boys burst out laughing. "Come now, we must go down to the cabins. It's getting cold in the wind and soon it will be time to eat."

It was July of 1838 when the two elder sons of the Rev. Andrew Murray, Sr. set sail for Scotland in the care of fellow passengers, Rev. and Mrs. James Archbell, Wesleyan missionaries homeward bound on furlough. The boys were to live at their uncle's home in Aberdeen, Scotland, to pursue their education.

The voyage was a miserable one. They didn't reach their destination until well into autumn. Questioned in later years as to what he remembered about the trip, Andrew candidly remarked, "Nothing at all except that Mrs. Archbell had a baby."

It is fortunate that memories fade with time, for the lad arrived in Scotland suffering from scurvy, prolonged seasickness, limited nutrition, and change of climate. Accustomed to sunny South Africa, the Murray boys found it difficult to adjust to bleak and wintry Scotland. They probably didn't fully grasp how long an entire decade would be—the length of time their parents arranged for their education abroad. It is often the Lord's mercy to veil the time required to reach a distant goal and force us to concentrate on one step at a time.

That first step for Andrew and John upon arrival in Scotland was to enroll in school the day after they set foot on non-swaying land. Uncle John, their father's brother, was a respected, conservative, strict but loving disciplinarian who didn't believe in wasting time. He was one of the keenest of the evangelical clergymen of his country, a serious scholar, and a deeply spiritual man. He influenced his brother, Andrew Murray, Sr., in much the same way as young John was to influence his brother Andrew with godly guidance and caring companionship.

Andrew Murray, Sr. had the utmost confidence to commit his sons to the care of his brother's family which consisted of uncle, aunt, one son and three daughters of about the same age as children of the Murray family in South Africa. It turned out to be a most happy though difficult seven years of preparation, leaving a lasting impression on every aspect of the boys' lives and characters.

How did it happen that one Scottish Murray brother, Andrew, was planted in a Dutch community in South Africa, and the other Murray brother, John, remained in the land of their birth, both serving as ministers? Why were the sons of the South African Murray pursuing their education so far away in the land of their father's birth? God's ways are mysterious but perfect.

In His sovereignty, God planned for South Africa to produce a son who, through his preaching and writing, would influence for Jesus Christ not only the land of his birth, but Europe and America and people of many nations for generations to come. It was this lad of ten, the young Andrew Murray, born on May 9, 1828, who was destined by God to speak to coming generations as few men are privileged to do. His name has become a household word in Christian homes and churches throughout the world through his 240 books and tracts in English and Dutch. His works have been published in more than fifteen languages.

The ancestors of the Murrays were associated with the Presbyterian Church of Scotland, a godly heritage. The immediate ancestors of Andrew Murray, Sr., the father of our biographical subject, were farmers in Aberdeenshire, Scotland. To sort them out becomes difficult because both his father and grandfather bore the given name of Andrew.

Andrew Sr.'s father died comparatively young, and on his deathbed he prayed aloud for his four children by name. John, one of the two boys, only twelve at the time, overheard his father's prayer, and the impression made on him was so deep that he dedicated himself to the service of Christ. He resolved to prepare for the ministry and assist his brother Andrew in his education. This he did, with the help of Almighty God.

Now history was repeating itself with another set of brothers in 1838 with the same names, the elder looking after the younger.

The favorite son of his widowed mother, Andrew Sr. warmly returned the affection of his mother, a woman of great beauty and lovableness. He tried to obey her in all matters. At the close of his college course he received an invitation to St. John's parish in Newfoundland but declined in order to remain near his mother.

But when another call came, he recognized it as from God and felt strongly that he must accept it. In spite of his tender love for his mother, he left her lying on what proved to be her deathbed without letting her know how distant was his destination—South Africa, considered the most remote corner of the world in those days.

As he waited for the stagecoach to take him away, he and his brother John committed one another to God's care and sang together the old hymn, O God of Bethel, which became the traditional family hymn of the widely scattered Murray households in generations to come.

O God of Bethel
(The Murray family hymn)

O God of Bethel, by whose hand
    Thy people still are fed,
Who through this weary pilgrimage
    Hast all our fathers led,

Our vows, our prayers, we now present
    Before thy Throne of grace;
God of our fathers, be the God
    Of their succeeding race.

Through each perplexing path of life
    Our wandering footsteps guide;
Give us each day our daily bread,
    And raiment fit provide.

O spread thy covering wings around
    Till all our wanderings cease,
And at our Father's loved abode
    Our souls arrive in peace.

> Such blessings from thy gracious hand
> Our humble prayers implore;
> And thou shalt be our chosen God,
> And portion evermore.
>
> *Stanzas 1–4 by Philip Doddridge, 1737*
> *Stanza 5 by John Logan, 1781*

Andrew Sr. studied Dutch in Holland for several months, then sailed for South Africa. He was never to see his brother again, but his sons would spend their formative years under their uncle's roof.

What prompted this strong call to the young Scotsman to cause him to choose it above prestigious pulpits in his fatherland? In 1652 the Dutch East India Company founded a settlement at the Cape of Good Hope although they did not plan to colonize the country. It was simply to be a convenient port of call between Holland and the East, a place to refresh the crews and obtain supplies. But as the population increased, the sturdy Dutchmen ignored the company's policy and established settlements inland to seek better living conditions. Devout men, they founded congregations in those scattered communities, and a strong Dutch Church took shape along patterns of the church in Holland. It also depended on the homeland for its supply of ministers.

After the British arrived in the early 1800s, supply of pulpits became even more difficult, compounded by the vast distances between the congregations. From the beginning, the Dutch Church was closely connected with the government. That situation persisted even after the arrival of the British. In all respects it was the national church of the country. The Governor of the Cape, Lord Henry Somerset, requested the Rev. Dr. George Thom, who came to South Africa in connection with the London Missionary Society, although a minister of the Dutch Church of Caledon, to try to recruit a supply of ministers from Scotland.

Andrew Murray, Sr., responded to his recruitment in 1821, the first of a number of able Scotsmen who heard the Macedonian cry for help and left their homeland for permanent ministry in Africa. Andrew Murray, Sr.'s, appointment upon arrival was the district of Graaff-Reinet.

There was significant unity between the two great Presbyterian Churches, that of Scotland and the Dutch Reformed Church of South Africa. The only difference was language, and Andrew Sr. soon mastered that. He learned to preach fluently in Dutch.

In his early thirties, Andrew Sr. still lacked something vitally important to his ministry—a wife. In Cape Town on a trip related to a synod meeting he met a beautiful young lady, Maria Stegmann, who married him the following year when she was only sixteen. She was not quite twenty when young Andrew, the subject of our story, was born. His mother's combined German, French Huguenot and Calvinist Dutch ancestry mingled with his father's pure Scottish blood to give Andrew a sturdy heritage.

Andrew Sr. so identified with the land of his adoption that his children could never remember hearing him express any longing to revisit Scotland. His parish, Graaff-Reinet, in which young Andrew spent the first ten years of his life, was and still is one of the most important towns in the Cape province. The congregation was founded in 1790, and for almost ninety years some member of the Murray family served the pulpit. Andrew Sr.'s pastorate extended over forty-four years. Graaff-Reinet is on a well-watered plain situated in the midst of the dry tableland called the Karroo, about 500 miles northeast of Cape Town and 140 miles north of Port Elizabeth.

Young Andrew's boyhood was a happy but disciplined one. The children were well trained in the ways of the Lord and obeyed their father without question. His word was law, from his decision there was no appeal, and his wisdom was never debated. This attitude carried over during the years his two sons were abroad. They consulted their father through correspondence and agreed with his every decision. It was a loving, willing obedience, by no means forced.

The elder Murray's conversations with his children were always purposeful. On rides into the countryside he instructed them about natural history or geography or other matters of the world. He made a point to speak to each of his children concerning their spiritual condition on appropriate occasions. Sometimes it was on Sunday evenings after family worship when the children came to him for a good-night kiss.

The older children were expected to be concerned for the spiritual welfare of the younger. Singing of hymns and memorization of Scripture were indelibly imprinted on the Murray children's memories.

Nor did Andrew forget his father's sacred Friday evening habit: he regularly devoted the whole time to prayer for revival. He would shut himself in his study and read accounts of former revivals in Scotland and other countries and often read stories to the family of the outpouring of the Holy Spirit on some particular church. Andrew vividly remembered standing outside the study door listening to his father's loud crying to God and pleading for a similar outpouring in his own parish, elsewhere in South Africa, and in the world.

Andrew Sr. lived to see some of his prayers answered. At a conference in Worcester in 1860, when the wave of blessing which was sweeping over America, Ireland, Scotland, and England began to reach the shores of Africa, he broke down in tears before the gathering when he spoke of his great longing for revival. Within a year the blessing came to his congregation.

Long before slavery was abolished, Andrew Sr. aligned himself with the cause of the slaves. It is important to note that in his own household he never employed any black person without first giving the individual his or her liberty and guaranteeing fair treatment and a good living standard.

Because Andrew's mother was so young, she was a close companion to her sons and daughters. She was known as a contented person, thoroughly happy in her husband, in her children, and supremely happy in the love of God. Rest and peace in the midst of much work was her hallmark. Communion with God was her secret. Children and servants knew that mother must not be disturbed when she shut her door for private devotions. She became the mother of eleven children, most of whom became ministers or married ministers, thus exerting a wide influence for Christ.

The Murray home was a crossroads for important persons in the Christian world since Graaff-Reinet was on the main road to the interior. The parsonage provided hospitality to many of the remarkable missionaries of those early days: Dr. Moffatt and Dr. Livingstone, the earlier French missionaries, and many from Scotland and Germany.

The two-level Murray manse was spacious, in every respect the finest residence in the village, finer than the house of the magistrate. It had a huge yard and outbuildings with a large garden of flowers, a vineyard and fruit trees. Indoors was an immense dining hall, drawing rooms, study, many bedrooms, connecting rooms with arches—all a delight for the children to play hide-and-seek with playmates who were always welcome. The parsonage habitually resounded with merriment. All was dedicated to the Lord, a haven to friend or stranger for physical and spiritual refreshment.

From such a large and godly family and thriving church environment, young Andrew was severed at the tender age of ten. A sensitive boy, he was described as "exuberant in spirit, less quiet than his brother in thought and speech, of a retentive memory and able easily to assimilate knowledge; not less earnest than his brother and devout from childhood." The two brothers were close companions during their formative years but were in many respects different. John favored his father—quiet, reserved, and cautious in word and deed. Andrew favored his mother in his features and character, with a bright and eager disposition.

The boys had a loyal affection for each other without jealousy or competitiveness. John frankly admired the talents of Andrew who, although two years younger, kept up with him all through their student years. Andrew admired John's steadiness of character and sober judgment. He tried hard to imitate John's diligence and good work habits.

Why was it necessary for the Murray boys to leave such an ideal environment? It was not common to send children abroad in the early 1800s because the distance to Europe was so great and separations would be long. No flying home for vacation breaks! But public education at that period in South Africa was at its lowest ebb because poor salaries did not attract high quality teachers. Little more than the basic three Rs were taught. Enterprising parents in some of the larger towns pooled their resources to hire a teacher who would at least instruct in Latin and mathematics. The Sr. Murrays were genuinely concerned about the education of their two elder sons, who showed great academic promise. After much thought and prayer, the parents decided to send their sons to Scotland. The separation was not easy for parents or children, but the youngsters proved mature enough to understand that it was for their highest welfare and motivated by the love of their parents.

Andrew saw the difficult separation in the proper perspective and respected and loved his parents for it. That he appreciated the foundation of love and spiritual nurture they invested in him is reflected in a memo to the entire Murray family circle scores of years later:

> A godly parentage is a priceless boon. Its blessings rest not only upon the children of the first generation, but have often been traced in many successive generations. But its blessings will depend upon the keeping up of the spirit of prayer, with that direct sense of belonging to God. When God blessed Abraham and his seed it was that through them all the nations of the earth were to be blessed. And so God still means that a family which He blesses should be the channel through which a neighborhood or a people shall learn to know Him.
>
> To belong to such a family implies high privilege, but equally high responsibility. The spirit of the world is so strong, the slackening of the spiritual life on the part of the parents comes in so easily, that unless the charge God has committed to us be jealously guarded, the inheritance may easily become spent and lost. It is well for a family to acknowledge what it owes to the prayers of its ancestors.

2

Sturdy Branches Spread

For all practical purposes, young Andrew and John were adopted into a new family for seven years. After having a happy and contented Mamma as their home's guiding light in Africa, they found their aunt a contrast in temperament. Often depressed and moody and without a buoyant spirit, she was nevertheless treated tenderly by Uncle John Murray who stood by her with comfort in her times of difficulty. To observe firsthand such a patient spirit in his saintly uncle caused Andrew in later years to write understandingly and with sympathy toward doubting and unsettled Christians.

A tribute to the boys' behavior under all circumstances was given by one of their cousins. "Their uncle and aunt never once had to find fault with either of the boys during their entire stay in our home. We, the younger members of the family, counted them as brothers and were brokenhearted when they left us."

The boys knew their parents were praying for them continually and counting on them to do their best so they applied themselves well to their studies. Another factor motivated them: the local lads and lassies had the distorted idea that anyone from Africa must be an utter savage, which included lads of the Colonies. Andrew and John tried to prove them wrong. They soon earned the respect of their peers through their ability in the main subject of the grammar school, Latin. Although the Murray boys received no previous formal instruction in Latin other than that given by their father, what they learned from him was equal to the level of the local students.

As the boys advanced into their teens and took the entrance exams at Marischal College, it was Andrew, then only thirteen, who qualified for a scholarship. The brothers continued on the same grade level throughout their academic preparation.

Their father lovingly and seriously kept close tabs on his sons through letters, and they reciprocated with a great deal of correspondence which has been preserved.

"My dear boys," he wrote, "you may both depend on it, though you are out of our sight you are seldom out of mind. We always follow you with our fervent prayers. . . . I trust you will ever remember that our having sent you abroad for study was for your own good. Had my affection for you swayed me to keep you here, you could never have seen or known the half of the good you are likely to see and know now. It will, however, under the blessing of God, depend much on yourselves whether or not the step we have taken shall be for your real benefit in this life and that which is to come."

He salted his letters with practical advice: "Try to keep as far up in your classes as you possibly can. Do your homework in the evenings and don't count on the morning hours before school too much. . . . Write often, everything about yourselves, your friends, your lodgings and studies. It will all be interesting to us and your friends and relatives here at home." With no airmail facility, letters back and forth took many months, as did the parcels which passed frequently between them.

Andrew deliberately held back one letter to his parents temporarily: "We delayed answering your letter, dear Papa and Mamma, because we wanted to see what our success might be at the end of the term. That success, however, has been very small. John has gotten *seventh* prize in mathematics!" Nevertheless, both boys did exceptionally well and received their share of honors and prizes during the seven years.

While the boys were in Aberdeen, the Free Church of Scotland was established in 1843, and fully a third of those in the Scottish state church pulled out. Thomas Chalmers, Robert Murray McCheyne and, in particular, the revivalist preacher W. C. Burns, who became a missionary to China in 1847, were largely responsible for the disruption.

At the same time, the religious climate in Scotland was verging on revival. Philanthropy, education, and religion were all claiming fresh attention. Politically, the Chartists were active. Under the inspiration of the great-hearted and saintly Dr. Thomas Chalmers, everything evangelical received new enthusiasm. Recognized as the greatest preacher of his time, attracting great crowds and resulting in the salvation of many, he had powerful influence on the church. He did not emphasize structural church planting as much as outreach with the Word—carrying the gospel to homes through visitation and witness.

Solid views regarding the inspiration of the Scriptures as the sole and supreme authority and rule of faith and morals also came to the fore at that time. Among the younger evangelicals were Dr. Candlish, McCheyne, the two Bonars, and A. N. Somerville. John and Andrew undoubtedly were present at the meetings of many of these godly men, especially in the great tent gatherings and mass meetings at which Dr. Chalmers preached to crowds of 6,000 to 10,000 people. It was said that everyone could clearly hear him without a public address system!

It was Andrew's assignment to read aloud to his Uncle John while the latter ate his dinner. By this wise arrangement many a thought from these great preachers was sown in the fertile soil of his keen young mind and would bear a harvest in his own preaching and writing in later years.

A remarkable spiritual awakening was taking place in Scotland similar to that stirring in America under Charles Finney. The man God used to implement it was the young Rev. William C. Burns, who was destined to have a great influence over both the Murray lads, especially over Andrew. Mr. Burns was described as "inexperienced, with slow speech, no particular gifts of charm or eloquence or winning sweetness. But he had about him such an air of divine commission that he could not be criticized and drew even careless people to receive him as a messenger of God." His few, plain words were full of weight and power, finding their mark directly in men's hearts because he spent much time in prayer and fasting. He was particularly effective in youth ministry.

Mr. Burns was often a guest in Uncle John's home so Andrew and John came into close contact with him. Andrew even had the dubious honor at age twelve to carry Mr. Burns' coat and Bible to church, which seems to have been some kind of coveted privilege. What Andrew saw of this man's genuine spiritual life, power with God, and public ministry, affected him deeply.

On one occasion after Mr. Burns left the city, he answered a letter young John wrote him. He used strong but loving words to warn him. "You are not excusable in remaining in your present unrenewed state. There really is not the smallest possible hope of your being saved unless you are really born of the Holy Spirit and reconciled to the Holy Jehovah by the atoning blood of His only begotten Son. Search your heart, my dear fellow-sinner. . . . Oh, dear friend, be not tempted to put off to a more convenient season your entire consecration to Emmanuel. . . ." He added a P.S. "Show this to Andrew to whom it may also apply. I'll answer his letter later."

Toward the end of their studies in Scotland, their father wrote the boys to begin serious thought and prayer about choosing their life vocations. He advised them not to take up some career which they could just as well have trained for by remaining in South Africa. That would defeat the purpose of sending them abroad for wider opportunities of study.

"I do hope you won't think of law, because our Bench and Bar in South Africa are corrupt. Should you feel inclined toward theology or medicine or business, I have no doubt there will always be openings at the Cape as well as in other places. If I were you, I'd at least be open to consider the Indian Missions—*there* is something worthy of the ambition of great minds. Even to enter education would be worthy. . . ."

Andrew's letter to his father must have crossed in the mail. In it he already informed his father that, after careful thought and prayer, he decided to give himself to the work of preaching the gospel.

His father answered, "I have now to congratulate you on your choice of a profession and rejoice that the Lord has been pleased to incline your heart the way He has done." He added a serious comment, "I trust, however, my dear boy, that you have given your heart to Jesus Christ to be His now and His forever, to follow Him through good and through bad report."

It appears that quite often in those days when the service of the Church was such a viable career choice and pursued by so many, that young men often entered the ministry without having been born again. The line between being brought up in a devout Christian environment, accepting Christianity as a matter of fact, as against a definite, personal decision of repentance and crisis of new birth, was a very indistinct line for some. It was perceptive of his father to draw this distinction. Young Andrew actually dated his personal conversion several years later.

The elder Murray went on to counsel his son: "The service in the church of South Africa does not promise you much wealth or ease in this world, but a field of usefulness as extensive as you could desire among a kind and indulgent people. . . . I would recommend that you study Divinity a year or two in the Free Church of Scotland, then go for a year or two to Holland, as much to acquire the Dutch language as for theology, and get licensed and ordained for the Church at the Cape."

The more reflective brother John seems to have taken longer to reach his decision to become a minister. His problem was mainly that he regarded the claims of the ministry as too exalted for his devotion and strength. After some indecision, and strong counsel from his Uncle John, to whom he was closer than was Andrew, he too decided to devote himself to theology.

In the spring of 1845 both brothers passed their final exams in the arts and graduated with an M.A. from Marischal College. Andrew was not quite seventeen. The next step was to start on the theological course in Holland. Three more years of study in God's classroom of preparation stretched before the young men.

3

The Chocolate Club

"When I went to Holland, they overcharged me because I didn't speak Dutch," warned Andrew's father in a letter before the boys left Scotland. "And watch out for their abominable customs of drinking gin and smoking tobacco and cigars. Entertain your friends with tea and coffee—Holland is famous for both. Don't be afraid to be different."

Their father went on to advise against certain theological teachings which were not based on the Bible. "Be sure not to neglect your daily study of the Holy Scriptures. Pray much for the guidance of the Holy Spirit."

The Murray brothers set sail from Scotland in June 1845 to enroll at the Academy of Utrecht, later called the State University. Because they arrived shortly before the beginning of summer vacation, they had time to get used to an alien environment. They could only speak English and very imperfect Dutch, so they attempted to get along in the student circles with Latin.

One of their new friends commented that upon first sight he did not know what to make of them: "There were two youths in somewhat strange garb walking along the streets with cheerful countenances and unassuming demeanor . . . and whether their Latin was classically pure, or even intelligible or endurable, is open to question. But it was sufficient and we understood one another."

The religious condition of Holland at that time was unfortunately deplorable. Rationalism from Germany was spreading, and pulpits were occupied by ministers who had no use for evangelical doctrine, although they were still bound to preach the Calvinistic theology of the Dutch Reformed Church. The Christian lives of laymen were weak, and most people assumed only a diluted form of Sunday religion.

Conversion was an antiquated word, and the Holy Spirit appeared to have been replaced by the spirit of the times. Strange views of "broad-minded" men were the order of the day. The professors and the courses to which the Murrays were exposed reflected the religious corruption. It was said of the theological professors that their lectures "tasted of long Gouda pipes."

What a poor climate to nurture two young men who were to influence their generation significantly for the evangelical faith! But the sovereign God countered that influence by bringing the Murray boys in contact with a unique group of sincere, spiritual, fellow Christian students.

One spiritual spark had leaped over from Switzerland and ignited some Christians in Holland who were hoping and praying for "seasons of refreshing from the presence of the Lord." At that time, the spiritual condition of Switzerland was even worse, if possible, than Holland.

Two Scottish laymen, Robert and James Haldane, burdened with the deadness of a church that was founded by Calvin, embarked on an evangelistic mission to Switzerland and started Bible readings for the theological students at Geneva. Through some of their converts and co-workers, their influence penetrated Holland and became known by its French name *Réveil* or Revival. It did not originate in church circles but in literary circles, being largely confined to the aristocratic and upper middle classes. Influenced by the *Réveil*, in 1843 some Christian students at Utrecht founded the society known as Zekor Dabar ("Remember the Word," in Hebrew) "to promote the study of the subjects required for the ministerial calling in the spirit of the Revival." This was the group that gave a warm welcome to the Murrays.

The meetings of the society were held once a week in rotation in the rooms of each member who would then serve as host. The study and discussion of theological subjects took up the first three hours, at nine o'clock extemporaneous orations were heard, ending at ten when simple refreshments of bread, butter, cheeses and beverages were enjoyed with open fellowship. It was the refreshments that labeled them from the outside in a derogatory way. Because the group avoided wine and liquor and drank only coffee, tea, and Dutch chocolate, they were dubbed "The Chocolate Club." Members were ridiculed by professors as too fanatical and fellow students refused to sit by such "pious fellows" in class or rub shoulders with them in the halls.

No hermit clique, the group spent much time in gospel outreach. They held makeshift Sunday Schools for poor children, Bible classes for working men, and instead of enjoying their own recreation time, the young men devoted it to visiting the poor and preaching the gospel. With a vision beyond their immediate locale, the society and the Murrays pioneered a missionary band which met twice a month to pray for and learn about missions. The group began to publish its own sixteen-page monthly mission magazine in Dutch during the time the Murrays studied in Holland.

There is a striking similarity between the Murray brothers and two other brothers more than a hundred years earlier. Another famous circle of young men met in one of the rooms of Lincoln College, Oxford, England, whose leaders were John and Charles Wesley. Although the results of the two groups were different, they shared the same spirit of intense earnestness, enthusiasm to live consistent Christian lives, to align doctrine and living, and to reach out in good works. Both groups met with ridicule and persecution from fellow students on campus.

To study in such an adverse religious environment can destroy the faith of some Christian students even in our day. But it can also have the opposite effect of strengthening faith, which was the case with the Murrays. The new intellectual atmosphere to which they were introduced and the conflict with well-educated people who took different theological views caused them to examine their own foundations of faith in Christ more closely. They came out stronger by recommitting themselves to their heritage of faith in the Bible.

It was at Utrecht in 1845 when Andrew was only seventeen that he experienced a great change in his life which he himself called his conversion. This despite the fact that he was already assured of God's call to enter the ministry as a vocation and was sincerely committed to Christian matters from his childhood. To him this conversion was a distinct event which he could date and pinpoint in location to the very house and room. It was no cataclysmic experience of the moment but a precise time of complete surrender to Christ from which he dated a new era of his life. This milestone launched his whole ministry and set his sights for scores of years to the service of his Lord.

Andrew's own words describe it in a letter of congratulations to his parents after they wrote him that a new child, another son, was born.

> And equal, I am sure, will be your delight when I tell you that I can communicate to you far gladder tidings, over which angels have rejoiced, that your son has been born again. In my previous letters and conversation you may have noted a stiffness in my speaking about such things, and even now I hardly know how to write. . . . For the last several years there has been a continual process in my spiritual life. It did bother me and held me back that I lacked some kind of deep sight of my sins, which many other people seemed to have, before I could be converted. At present I can say I am confident that as a sinner I have cast myself on Christ. . . . Dear Parents, praise the Lord with me. . . . I am peaceful and have true confidence in God though my feelings of joy and prayer are not always consistent. My heart at present is warm, yet whenever I begin to write or speak, I fail. . . . I have a long way to go before I can do nothing but praise Him fully and continually. . . . Oh, that I might receive grace to walk more holy before Him!

The tone of his letters to his parents noticeably changed to continual praise and genuine enthusiasm for Christ and his personal part in God's work. In writing of the missionary prayer meeting of the Chocolate Club, Andrew refers to their interceding, together with Christians everywhere, "for the outpouring of God's Spirit on the world."

He began to think about further theological education in Germany after his Holland studies because "the lectures here are such that it is almost impossible to get any good from them." Besides, he reasoned in letters to his father, he would be only twenty years old at his graduation and under age for ordination. "And the living standard is cheaper in Germany," he added as an incentive. As much as Andrew longed to do this, he submitted himself to his father's wisdom whether both he and John should return to Africa after graduation.

The answer came back from Papa. Although Andrew could probably not be ordained before the age of twenty-two, there would be plenty of openings for usefulness to the Lord after his return, and it would be better for Andrew to get some experience before he had the full responsibility of a congregation. In fact, he hinted of "mission type" challenges right within South Africa which should appeal to any earnest, young Christian worker.

Andrew replied that his full desire was to place himself in God's hands to be used wherever God chose, even if it was to return immediately to Africa and forego more European education. "Because an additional stock of human wisdom often proves nothing else than obstruction in God's way." At the same time, Andrew confessed that it was one of his natural weaknesses to be quite nonchalant about God's leading, with a certain indifference and contentedness as to the future, rather than having a strong, active burden of concern for God's work. But the zeal and burden that he felt he lacked came more completely with maturity and Andrew's full baptism in the Holy Spirit in later years.

During one of their long vacations, the Murray boys set off on an enjoyable walking tour of the Rhine Valley where they met a Pastor Blumhardt.

Through him they were exposed for the first time to a remarkable work for the demon possessed and healing of the sick by faith. This movement was to lead into a great revival in the Rhenish provinces.

Seeing for himself the reality of God's continuing miracles, Andrew's convictions about the validity of the power of God being available even today were firmly established. He wrote with firsthand knowledge and conviction in these areas in later years.

Prayer and intercession were prominent themes in Andrew's writings in his maturity. His conviction was based in part on his appreciation for the prayers of his parents while he and John were separated from them. In his books about godly child training, this spirit is likewise reflected.

He wrote to his parents, "I am sure we have often reaped the fruits of your believing prayers even while we were still unacquainted with true prayer. I trust we may still go on to experience what a blessing praying parents are. . . . May God grant you a rich answer to the many prayers you have offered for us by abundantly blessing your own souls."

On Andrew's twentieth birthday, May 9, 1848, The Hague Committee broke tradition and ordained both John and Andrew. The farewell gathering for the Murray boys was a deeply emotional affair for the Chocolate Club, with Bible readings, extended prayers, singing, and celebrating holy communion together. The group crowded around them singing Psalm 134, weeping and embracing the brothers whom they had grown to love so dearly. John pronounced the benediction, and at half past ten the boys climbed into a waiting carriage which was to take them to Vreeswijk and the voyage home.

The Murrays made a farewell visit to their uncle's home in Aberdeen, and the two boys were given the honor of preaching in his church. The family and congregation who knew them since their arrival as scarcely more than children had a hard time to decide "which of the two laddies was the grander preacher."

Andrew's preparation in Holland was a deeply significant period in his life. He formed habits of self-evaluation in those student years which developed his gracious Christian character and his fruitful ministry.

His broad theological and social contacts, as well as the continued companionship of his serious brother, left him a legacy of mature judgment and thoughtful temperament. Andrew was known for his exuberant spirit as a young man and his more conservative older brother often scolded him, "Andrew, you shouldn't laugh so much—that's not good," no doubt reflecting the spirit of their times that religion and joy should not be joined. In Andrew's later writings, however, they were not only linked but wedded.

4

God's Wilderness Classroom

At last—home in South Africa after ten years! The Murray boys left as children and their return as two young ministers from Europe was an event of more than local importance. It was announced in church magazines, referred to in the newspapers, and discussed in ecclesiastical circles throughout the country.

Papa and Mamma Murray could not be at Cape Town to meet the boys, but grandparents and other relatives were on hand to enthusiastically welcome them. Young as they were, they were invited to preach in established pulpits.

The first text on which Andrew preached was "We preach Christ crucified." "May it be true!" wrote Andrew to his parents. "But I feel it very difficult not to preach *myself*. I am afraid that I attend too much to beauty of thought and language and feel too little that God alone can teach me to preach." Andrew need not have feared, because God was getting ready to launch a new life-classroom experience for him in his first appointment out in the "wilderness" where he would learn that his "beauty of thought and language" would count for nothing!

But first came that longed-for visit to his home at Graaff-Reinet and reunion with parents and siblings, some of whom he had never seen. Apparently Andrew's boyish and playful disposition was so outstanding that he captured the hearts of his younger brothers and sisters. "Is brother Andrew *really* a minister?" they cried. "That can never be. He's just like one of us!"

But Andrew proved to be a serious-minded minister. On the first Sunday home, the two sons of the manse shared their father's pulpit. We wonder what their feelings were. Those who heard them were deeply impressed—the younger had such an earnestness and passion, the elder had a great thoughtfulness and incisiveness. At the communion table the father and sons officiated together.

When it was Andrew's turn to serve the elements and speak briefly, he rose, closed his eyes, and seemed lost in meditation and prayer. An almost painful hush fell upon the great congregation. When he finally spoke after a long interval, the words were evidently so sincere, so intense and uplifting that tears broke out all over the assembly. Could this man of God be the same boy of ten who left for Scotland a decade ago? The deep conviction was shared by all that a destiny from God rested upon this youth to impress his generation for Christ.

Appointments for service in the church at that time were totally in the hands of the Governor of Cape Colony, Sir Harry Smith. First the interviews, then the decisions: John was given charge of the parish at Burgerdorp, an honorable and coveted appointment. For Andrew? "I'm afraid I shall have to send you to Bloemfontein."

Thus Andrew became the pastor of a territory of nearly 50,000 square miles, including 12,000 people in a remote and unattractive parish beyond the Orange River. He was the first regular minister to live and work among the "voortrekkers," the hardy Dutch pioneers—backwoods people. Andrew started out on a mission field!

Comparing the size of Andrew's parish with his brother John's, someone facetiously remarked, "Since they could not place him as a minister, they made him a bishop."

Andrew Murray's life can only be fully understood with some background knowledge of the Dutch Reformed Church and its branch in South Africa. The Dutch settlement and the church were founded simultaneously in 1652, kept alive through preaching and sacraments administered by voyaging clergymen passing the Cape.

During the Dutch rule, the South African church was regarded as an integral part of the church in Holland, under its control, supplied by its ministers, and paid by a paternal government. By tradition, religion was severely unemotional and chiefly a form, with little impression on the everyday life of its communicants. The church was part of the civil establishment and ministers were government servants.

When the British rule began, theoretically the Dutch Reformed Church there was severed from its mother church in the Netherlands. But not until 1843 was a church ordinance passed which fully recognized the church's right to her own control without government interference. This was carried out with tension, difficulty, and dissatisfaction on both sides.

Thousands of farmers, Dutch Reformed Church members, were sour on British rule and in a "Great Trek" took off with their wives and children to new horizons in the territories north of the Orange River, known thereafter as the Orange Free State, the Transvaal, and Natal. Motivations were complex, not just religious. A fierce debate resulted as to whether or not the emigrants who had passed across the borders of the Colony were free from their allegiance to the British. On one side, the emigrants felt the long arm of the British reaching after them; on the other side, there were clashes with tribesmen.

One of the Cape governors in 1848 proclaimed the Queen's authority over the whole country between the Orange and Vaal rivers and annexed it under the title of the Orange River Sovereignty.

Battles of troops and emigrants followed until rebellion was at least driven underground. It was into this raw, pioneer situation that Andrew Murray plunged when he was appointed minister of Bloemfontein, the rustic pasture-capitol of the new Sovereignty.

It was customary for the parish which called a minister to fetch him in some manner. A huge wagon drawn by a team of powerful horses was dispatched to bring youthful Andrew from Graaff-Reinet to his new parish, a journey of 300 miles. Accompanied by his father, all his worldly possessions, and an escort of fifty young men on horseback, friends of Andrew, the entourage set off like a parade.

Besides his appointment as minister of Bloemfontein, Andrew was also to be acting minister of the adjoining parishes of Riet River (Fauresmith), Rietpoort (Smithfield), and Winburg. At each place the father presented his minister-son to his new congregation with an impressive ceremony. As a six-foot, slim, clean-shaven young cleric, he must have aroused many questions in the minds of seasoned, hardy, Dutch pioneers. Were his shoulders broad enough to carry such heavy responsibilities? Andrew had just celebrated his twenty-first birthday, and the extreme youth of this beardless boy made one old farmer exclaim: "Why, he is just like a little girl!"

As the father left his young son, barely in manhood, he took hold of the hands of the two elders and placed his son's in them. He requested, "Deal gently with the young man." The task which faced Andrew was to minister Christ over a vast area, a wild country full of wild animals (lions, leopards, and vicious wild dogs) and yet wilder men—turbulent emigrants and cruel dwellers of the veld.

The distances between Andrew's outposts were great. Helicopters, Land Rovers, and four-wheel-drive jeeps were not invented yet. Most of his time was taken up in travel over all kinds of roads, in all kinds of weather, by horseback or ox wagon. The "express speed" of the latter was clocked at two miles per hour! Roads were mere tracks in the wilderness, ruts from wagons carrying merchandise from the coast to inland villages. Bridges were few and fording was more common at low points. During downpours or in the rainy season, the roads were churned to mud. Flooding rivers often made it necessary for travelers to simply wait until waters abated. Farms were few, sometimes twenty or more miles apart, with a hundred or more miles between villages.

Most outlying farmers could come to church only four times a year. When they traveled to one of the larger villages for supplies, they planned their trip to coincide with the local, quarterly, sacramental service. On such a weekend the minister would hold up to nine services, among them examination for confirmation of youth, marriages, baptisms, and communion services. People coming to such a center would live in their wagons or tents while loading up with enough supplies for several months.

Andrew zealously galloped his circuit, interested in the spiritual welfare not only of the privileged but of the underprivileged. He started Sunday School classes and Bible classes in efforts to reach even the Hottentots and Bushmen. "We have plenty of scholars," observed Andrew, "but no teachers."

He did not believe in merely allowing his church membership candidates to go through the forms or repeat the right answers. He insisted on thorough teaching on a long-term basis, spending many hours with each candidate seeking to discover true motives for wanting to be received into the church and evaluating the spiritual condition of each.

Contrary to tradition, he rejected many "on account of their defective knowledge. Others were lacking in earnestness and were really not seeking to believe in Christ."

At the communion services in Bloemfontein the number of communicants was so large that six tables had to be ministered to, each with separate hymn and address. Without a sufficiently large meeting hall, some of the gatherings took place under the open sky.

Andrew made one of his first trips across a plain known to be infested with wild dogs. His purpose was to reach a certain meeting about seventy miles distant. After fording a certain river and alighting from his horse to let it rest and graze, the horse suddenly caught the scent of dogs approaching and galloped off. Andrew calmly lifted his pack on his shoulders and began a walk of about fifteen miles to the nearest home.

The surprised farmer could not believe that he had escaped the fierce dogs and arrived alive. "How did you do it?"

The calm answer was, "I knew I was in the path of duty, so I prayed to God to protect me and walked straight on. Yes, the wild dogs snapped at me but did not touch me."

Andrew's characteristic attitude was to take things cheerily as they came because they were from the hand of God. Sometimes his meetings were in a church, sometimes at a gathering of tents and wagons, sometimes in the open air, even in the moonlight or in the dark with candles lighted only during the singing. Often he traveled at night in order to reach another group by early morning.

His burning love for the Lord and intense earnestness for the spiritual welfare of his people caused him much heart-searching. "When I look at my people, my peace forsakes me. . . . I tremble at the thought of my people's personal accountabilities for refusing my messages. . . . I am obliged simply to flee to the Master I serve and seek for a new and more entire surrender to His work. . . . Oh! that the coming year of my ministry may see me more and more a *minister of the Spirit*."

Andrew's overwhelming schedule took its toll. Without time to rest between discharging his enormous duties, the strong and healthy young man became worn out physically. He wrote his father, "I trust I shall be continually supported by your prayers. Oh! I care little whether I have strength enough or not, if only my own soul were but in a fitter state for commencing such a solemn work. Oh! for the anointing of the Spirit for my unclean lips, and His softening and enlightening and renewing grace for all who hear!"

5

Vacations for Spiritual Trek

As if his own 50,000 square mile parish were not large enough to fully challenge his efforts, young Andrew's missionary heart was burdened for the 7,000 emigrant farmers who wandered still further north beyond the Vaal River into the area known as Transvaal. Their children lacked education, secular and spiritual, and the farmers had no opportunity for the sacraments of the church or to hear the Word of God.

Andrew was not authorized by his appointment to spend any of his prescribed parish time in such outreach. Therefore, although desperately needing physical refreshment himself, he invested his six weeks annual holidays to go over the Vaal on strenuous mission trips. To compound the difficulties, it was the rainy season, there were no roads, and sometimes up to fourteen hours in the saddle were required between outposts. Often he conducted forty services among the six scattered stations. When preaching to the nomadic and unsettled farmers, he held meetings in the open and under tent sails spread from wagon to wagon.

Early on the first tour he caught what seemed at first to be only a chill; later a fever that continued off and on throughout the trip. The deacon accompanying him apparently suffered from the same symptoms as Andrew and died when he reached home. The Delagoa Bay fever was suspected as it was spreading with alarming rapidity throughout the Transvaal. Andrew lay for many weeks very near death in a tent instead of a hospital, attended by old Dutch ladies who loved and almost worshiped him. He recovered, but the sickness had been extremely hard on him. He was described by a friend, "instead of a strong, healthy, rosy-faced man six feet tall, he seemed to have shrunk into a bag of mere skin and bones and looked like a living skeleton."

When he returned to Bloemfontein, a doctor told him, "I am afraid you will never preach again. Be content to spend your life on a sofa." But God had only begun to work His image in Andrew Murray.

Beside the obvious spiritual successes of his ministry in the Transvaal, his trips there had far-reaching importance relating to political issues. The Transvaal settlers were highly suspicious of ministers of the Dutch Reformed Church because they were appointed by the governor and paid from public funds. These rebellious farmers wanted little to do with anything that smacked of British control or the "establishment," and that included a young minister who answered to a British colonial governor.

But Andrew's earnest zeal and genuine love and care for the welfare of these emigrants knit their hearts to him. They saw that he brought them ministrations of God's grace at the cost of great physical impairment to himself. His influence went so far as to restore some of their confidence in the Cape Dutch Reformed Church and even fostered a desire to remain a part of that ecclesiastical communion.

Andrew made two further vacation visits to the Transvaal and so endeared himself to the people that they begged for him to be assigned to their territory as his parish. They petitioned the church councils again and again to release Andrew for this wilderness pastorate. His heart longed to accept but he was neither allowed to, nor did it appear to be the will of God for his ministry at that time. But because of his great burden for those people and for the thousands in his own parish, he continued to expend himself, literally galloping from one preaching session to another.

He reflected in a letter, "It sometimes makes me unhappy to think that I must preach God's Holy Word with so little preparation, and though circumstances prevent my studying much, yet I long to live much more in a state of mind which would be a continual preparation. Oh! could I but live more in heaven, breathing the spirit of God's Word, the Lord would abundantly make up the lack of regular study."

Andrew's training in Scotland under the scholarly and spiritual guidance of his uncle gave him an excellent background to grasp the significance of the times and to be in a mentally alert position to mold current events to spiritual ends. This made him a power for good in his own country on many levels, not only in the religious field.

He was genuinely concerned with the welfare of the people in the Orange River Sovereignty when a protest was launched, after much debate and upheaval among the people, against the decision of the British government to abandon the country. Andrew had been an integral part of the official proceedings and involved in the committee matters to the extent that he and Dr. A. J. Frazer, an army surgeon who had settled down in the Sovereignty, were chosen as delegates to go to England to lay before the Ministry an extensively signed petition against abandonment.

Andrew was pulled in both directions. Should he decline the appointment or go if there was a possibility of doing his country a service? His declined health was another reason for considering a leave because his extreme weakness dragged on. He described it as "a weakness in my back, legs, and arms, with a sort of nervous trembling in my hands." He felt that perhaps the long voyage with the benefit of sea air and a change of pace might help to restore him. He was twenty-five at the time. After much prayer and consultation with his family, he decided to go and sailed in January 1854.

Before they landed in England, events had taken dramatic turns back in South Africa. Articles were signed at a convention in Bloemfontein that guaranteed in the fullest sense the independence of the country, finally freeing them from allegiance to Britain. The Orange River Sovereignty was changed into the Orange Free State, fortunately unaccompanied by bloodshed. Thus the mission of Dr. Frazer and Andrew was a lost cause which they had to abandon. As an unfortunate by-product, the political implications of the trip caused considerable suspicion against him in his home country.

While Andrew was in London, people began to take notice of his fame as an earnest and deeply spiritual young preacher, and he was offered many preaching engagements, even invited to occupy the pulpit of the noted Surrey Chapel. Knowing that he should not expend himself because of his health, and longing for a rest, he wrote to his sister, "Perhaps I ought not preach at all. But I find it difficult to refuse since preaching is, in fact, most refreshing to myself."

He spent some time in Holland and Scotland, hoping to find young men willing to go to South Africa as ministers and teachers. He had no success in finding such men, and his conviction grew clearer and more urgent that South Africa needed to establish a theological seminary of its own to fill the need for trained men.

While he was in Scotland, his health further deteriorated. "I feel my strength so worn that I do not believe that even perfect rest for three or four months would restore me, and a single summer in Africa would lay me prostrate. The doctor says that my whole system has been much more seriously affected than I have any idea, and prolonged rest is necessary to restoration. He advises that I should not leave before winter. . . . What I chiefly suffer from is the pain in my hands and arms. Half an hour's lively conversation, or earnest application to anything that requires thinking, immediately makes itself felt there. I cannot even write a note without feeling the pain in my arms. . . ."

As it turned out, he was obliged to be absent from South Africa for a year and nine months. God was perfecting the timing of the next great event He planned for His young servant.

6

A Bride Prepared

"There will be another guest at the table tonight, my dear," announced Howson Edward Rutherfoord to his wife, who was always as eager as her husband to show hospitality to God's servants.

"Is it a minister?" Mrs. Rutherfoord questioned, as her young daughter Emma entered the room and tuned in to the conversation.

"Indeed, and a young one at that, to whom I've taken quite a fancy," he added with a twinkle in his eye and a glance toward his lovely daughter. "He has just returned from England."

Emma picked up her needlework but became intensely interested. "Is he English, Papa? How old is he? Is he handsome?"

- - - - -

God in His sovereign plan had been preparing two lives who were to become one in marriage and in service to God, who would leave a legacy of generations of godly men and women. We have followed Andrew's early years. Now we will meet Emma, next to the eldest daughter of the Rutherfoords, an English family who adopted South Africa as their home. Mr. Rutherfoord came to Cape Town in 1818 as a businessman. He soon became successful and raised his family in fairly comfortable circumstances. He was further known for his civil contributions, his generosity, and association with the worthy cause of the Cape of Good Hope Society established for aiding deserving slaves and children of slaves to purchase their freedom.

How can we learn the intimate thoughts and enter into the life of someone who was born in 1835? We are fortunate that during her lifetime Emma wrote thousands of letters to her family and especially to her sister. That treasure is preserved in the Murray family archives. Emma "comes to life again today, young and fresh and wholesome, from a bundle of old, old letters" as her granddaughter, Joyce Murray, wrote in two books of Emma's compiled correspondence.

The granddaughter admitted to finding it difficult to read her young grandmother's letters because of her "bad handwriting, which was a family joke. The letters consisted often of odd sheets, sometimes sixteen pages long, filled with close, pointed Victorian handwriting in which the 'loops' of one line mix with those of the lines above and below. Moreover, in the mode of the times Emma indulged in long bouts of moralizing, pompous phrases, sometimes seeming stilted to present-day ears. As she poured out her joys and troubles and inmost thoughts to her elder sister, Mary, who lived in India, one may have the uncomfortable feeling of being an eavesdropper on a private conversation," wrote the granddaughter. "But we should not feel guilty about reading over Emma's shoulder because most of her letters were freely circulated in her family."

Emma grew up in comparative luxury in the large Rutherfoord home in the suburb of Cape Town at Sea Point. The grounds ran down to the sea, while behind the house stretched the slopes of a mountain. The children had a large garden as their playground and nearly two miles of rocky beach. The family had plenty of indoor and outdoor servants who had to be supervised. When Emma was not quite eighteen, and after her sister Mary was married and no longer in the household, her mother delegated to Emma the duties of the eldest daughter.

Emma accompanied her mother in the carriage when she paid calls on friends and helped her receive their many visitors. The family was noted for its generous hospitality to missionaries of every society and denomination, although the Rutherfoords continued as members of the Church of England, Holy Trinity Church on Harrington Street. Emma was taught how to give out the household stores each morning to the servants, keep the weekly household accounts, and be an example to her younger sisters. She learned to supervise routine housekeeping, plan meals and keep tradesmen's accounts. Apparently she did not do much cooking since that was delegated to domestic help.

The daughters of the family were educated at home by visiting governesses and masters who taught them traditional Victorian accomplishments of music, drawing, fancy work, and a smattering of French and German. Emma also took up the study of the Dutch language and wrote that she didn't expect much difficulty in picking up enough to speak. Little did she know Dutch would be her main medium of communication in her future husband's parishes.

Emma was a girl of broad literary background, brought up doing an enormous amount of serious reading under the supervision of her mother. Evenings were spent together as a family. The women would do fancy needlework while someone read aloud, or they listened to music which they performed themselves. She mentioned the excitement of reading *Uncle Tom's Cabin* by Harriett Beecher Stowe which was creating a worldwide sensation and just became available at the Cape. She wrote her sister, "By this year [1853] over a million copies have been published and as an international best-seller it eclipsed all previous records except perhaps the Bible. Papa is enchanted with it and reads it morning, noon, and night."

Dickens was the favorite author of her brother Frederic, but Emma didn't share his interest. "Dickens' stories are too long and trifling." She wrote of the family reading aloud the life of Madame Guyon. Emma had many opportunities to listen to her parents and their friends discussing current events, politics, and opinions and developed intelligent interest in many matters of the world. When Andrew first met her, he found her mature beyond her years.

Her main activities outside the home were visiting, distributing tracts, and teaching in a little church school. She enjoyed walking (called "pedestrianism," a Victorian term), hiking, even some mountain climbing. She was fond of horseback riding and was quite able to hold her own in physical activities of the day. Drawing or sketching was one of Emma's interests and she wrote frequently of coming across beautiful scenery which she longed to sketch. Seascapes, mountains, her home, garden and favorite buildings were among the objects of her art work.

The children of the family had a variety of pets including several small dogs to whom they taught tricks. She wrote about one called "Thistle" that her sister Ellen taught to sit up while holding something on its nose. "It is so ridiculous, but he is a very apt pupil." She also kept canaries, rabbits, and carrier pigeons as pets.

Gardening was not simply a leisurely pastime because vegetables and fruit trees were essential to provide the family with fresh produce. The whole family pitched in with gardening. When the family later moved to Herschel, their home was in the center of an area famous for well-laid-out gardens and orchards. Emma's mother delighted in collecting ferns and bulbs and shrubs from the surrounding countryside and imported many from overseas, especially new varieties of fruit trees. She belonged to the newly formed Botanical Garden Commission. Emma grew prize roses, and that interest carried over to whatever parish the Murrays served throughout their lifetime.

When Emma was barely twenty, her best friend Janie married, and Emma was her bridesmaid. She wrote to her sister:

> It makes me feel quite old to see all my companions married, but they are all older than I am. I am sorry to lose their company, but I should be more sorry to follow their example, for I'm sure I'm not fit for marriage, and am very happy as I am.
>
> Mama says it requires more character to be a worthy old maid than a married lady. I am afraid to tell her for fun that I do not have a good enough character to be an old maid. Mama seems in constant fear that I will leave the household and tells me I shall break her heart if I do, and Papa will never laugh again. I comfort her by saying I see no prospect of such a calamity. So, dear sister, you may always direct my letters "Miss Rutherfoord" to the end of my days.
>
> It is true many girls here waste their time and minds by too quickly falling in love, but the fault is in their lack of education and not having better things set before them. . . . I wouldn't ever want to leave

the dear old Cape. Here I have so much to do and so many things to interest me that it would be a long time before I could be happy to settle elsewhere. Besides, I don't like moving about. Oh, a short trip here and there for holidays is fine, but it seems as though my sphere of usefulness lies here.

How soon she would be proved wrong in all of those matters!

Emma assumed a bit of superior air as she commented on "girls who were bent on trifles and follies and vanities of dress." However, when the dressmaker arrived at the Rutherfoord home on occasion, it was definitely an event she enjoyed. She was as excited as the next girl to have a new frock for Christmas or some special event. A Victorian dress with all its bonings, paddings, flounces, etc., was a work of art and not to be taken lightly.

Paper patterns had only recently become popular. All the women looked forward to the monthly English edition of the *Domestic Magazine* and gladly paid the two pence. The latest fashions were discussed when ladies gathered for tea. *Mrs. Beeton's Book of Household Management*, sort of a bible of everything a Victorian woman needed to know about running her home, was read from cover to cover by most English women in South Africa.

Emma enjoyed a warm, close relationship with her father. He gave his children much attention and provided the best education of the day for them. Emma wrote, "Papa has the habit of looking into our rooms to see what we are doing. It puts me in a fright for fear my room should not be tidy. But he says he doesn't come in to check on that, and only walks in to give us each a kiss and disappears. He told us on our walk last evening that we children were worth our weight in gold."

Into the happy, settled life of this mid-Victorian young lady who was scarcely out of her teens entered a young minister. Rev. Andrew Murray, Jr., as he always signed himself, arrived on the scene with a package of emotional complications for Emma. He had just returned from England where he was sent on church business related to the Orange River Sovereignty in the company of Dr. A. J. Fraser. Andrew had stayed abroad longer than planned, hoping the change of climate might help restore his health. Dr. Philip, the Secretary of the London Missionary Society in Cape Town, introduced him to Emma's father who invited him at once to the family home at Herschel. At this point we resume our love story. . . .

The mystery dinner guest was about to arrive, and Emma was curious to hear all about him. Her parents laughed. "He is one of the noted Murray sons of the Graaff-Reinet parish. About twenty-seven years old, I imagine. Yes, handsome, but quite on the thin side. Perhaps some good Rutherfoord cooking would fatten him up!" Mr. Rutherfoord chuckled.

Apparently the food and the companionship drew Andrew to accept repeated invitations to dinner at their suburban Cape Town home. The entire, well-educated household took to him immediately because of his wide cultural interests and energetic personality. They described him as "a good talker yet always ready to listen." But it was lovely Emma with whom he would stroll in the garden at twilight.

Andrew was sure he had found the bride he was looking for, but unfortunately he moved too fast. It was love at first sight for him. Being an impulsive young man and quite accustomed to getting what he wanted, he decided to marry Emma immediately and take her back with him to Bloemfontein. Whoa!

Emma, although she found him attractive, was not to be swept off her feet. She wanted time to think about such an important, lifelong decision. Things had to be done decently and according to custom. Andrew's haste apparently shocked her dignity and her sense of what was fitting to her social position and sensitivities. That her father was immediately delighted when Andrew asked permission to marry his daughter did not influence her.

Poor Andrew. How was he to know that the timing of his proposal was unfortunate for many reasons. Emma and her sister Ellen had been spending much time and excitement arranging a Christmas Tree party for the fifth birthday party of the young son of the aide-de-camp to the governor. This was apparently a major social occasion at the Cape. "The tree was splendid with tapers, sugar plums and flowers, and the party was to include a most elegant supper." Even the governor of the Cape and his wife were to attend. Moreover, this was one of the first Christmas trees anyone had seen at the Cape. Certainly not one decorated and lit in June—no problem for the doting parents of the boy. It seems that Andrew's hasty proposal so annoyed both Emma and Ellen that at the last minute they were too upset even to go to the party on which they had spent so much time and effort. Let's listen to Emma pouring out her heart in a letter to her sister:

> A young clergyman of much promise connected with the Dutch Church came to our house about a month ago, where he has rather frequently been, and lately even staying with us. I thought he left for his parish in the interior yesterday, but he returned most unexpectedly and found me alone. He communicated something to me then that I was completely unprepared for, that surprised me. I was speechless, totally unable to reply to him. I spent all morning drafting a refusal. What do you think of it, dear sister?
>
> "Dear Sir, It was with feelings of perfect astonishment and wonder that I [heard your marriage proposal] yesterday. My feelings quickly changed to deep pain and regret. A proposal of marriage after so short an acquaintance has shocked me. How can there be mutual understanding and clear knowledge of one another's characters necessary for so close, so holy a relationship in so short a time? I feel obliged to decline any further acquaintance with you, but wish you a safe journey and much prosperity in your future labors.
>
> Believe me, Emma Rutherfoord."
>
> [Believe me is apparently the Victorian term for Sincerely yours, commonly used to sign letters.]
>
> His conduct to that point had been such as to put me perfectly at ease. I entertained such a respect for his character and felt that his mind was no ordinary one. Now his lack of consideration for me has wounded me most painfully. I don't even know his real character, and he is certainly a stranger to mine. Besides, even if I loved him with all my heart, it would be a bitter trial and great sacrifice to leave such a home as mine and enter a field of much hardship and self-denial. He never seemed to have thought of that.
>
> I would need a love surpassing anything I have yet known to keep me from fainting under the trials and sorrows of wedded life. Yes, I do think I am capable of that kind of love, and therefore I will never marry anyone till I feel it awakened. You must write and tell me what you

think about it all. Our sister Lucy is angry with me and will scarcely speak to me, because she has great affection for this Mr. Murray and thinks I ought immediately to have accepted his proposal. But how unkind I would be were I to marry him if I do not love him.

His sudden proposal so upset me that I locked myself in my room and I completely missed that spectacular, wonderful Christmas Tree party.

Mr. Murray called on Papa today to find out if my negative answer was final. I don't know what Papa told him. It is so sad that one whose mental superiority and whose work is all I could desire should be so lacking in heart cultivation. Time must heal both him and me. You can be sure I will not write any more on this subject. It is to your ear alone I ventured to pour out all this.

Apparently dear Emma felt that our Andrew was not romantic enough. Or perhaps too impulsive, too businesslike and too practical? After promising her sister that she wouldn't write about this brash young man ever again, in a follow-up letter to Mary she wrote:

Mr. Murray called on Papa once more before he left and admitted his conduct toward me had been very wrong and did not seek to excuse it. He expressed extreme regret. But he gave as reasons for his haste that his mind had been very harassed and pressed because the people of his church constantly urged his quick return. He only promised to leave them for ten months and had been absent twenty. Moreover he was pained at his entirely lonely condition with no one to associate with or be a companion.

Papa said Mr. Murray was evidently agitated and his mind overpressed. He said he felt my attitude was entirely proper and just, and it only heightened his esteem for me. He begged to be allowed to send me his very best regards, and so our acquaintance has ended. Whether we shall ever meet again is something I do not wish to think about now. At the same time, I am not quite happy with the way it is turning out. Papa and Mama have such an extremely high opinion of him, while I am so undecided.

I think what troubles me is that he seemed so businesslike in a matter of love and marriage. Something is missing. I don't know what exactly, perhaps a refinement of heart. I don't think I could ever marry without it. Especially were I to embark on living a difficult missionary life. I don't know whether this is the path God has appointed for me. I don't think I'm fitted for such a pioneer life. . . . Yet, with a man of warm heart as well as intellectual education, such a life could be a blessed one, a most happy one. . . .

I do trust Mr. Murray will get a good wife, a real companion, and a helpmeet. He may pick and choose from all the young ladies in town, Dutch or English, for they adore him. Perhaps I have done him some good and taught his heart a little. Perhaps next time he falls in love he will act in a different manner. . . . At the same time I have rather a dread for myself, to speak the truth, of becoming moss-grown and dank and slimy and rusty before my time with wasted powers. . . . I think it were better to wear out in an adventurous life than rust out, confined to a narrow and still narrowing home circle like some others I have observed.

Well, now I am going to dismiss Mr. Murray entirely from my thoughts. If God means it to be, it will be, and no thinking upon it now can do good. I want to keep my judgment unbiased and my heart free, and then leave everything to God. Now farewell to this subject.

But Mr. Murray out-of-sight was not Mr. Murray out-of-mind. While insisting to her sister that she would no longer think or write about the matter, her letters were permeated with the struggles of her heart. "I am trying to think of nothing but the present day and its duties, yet I seem to be moving in the midst of clouds, like dreaming, though all looks bright around me."

She seemed to be continually thinking of Andrew's good points, the conversations of the mind they shared, their reading of books together, their happy laughter, the sharing of his dreams for his ministry with her—symptoms of a young woman in whose heart were the stirrings of love. She eagerly followed the newspaper accounts of Andrew's return to Bloemfontein and the warm welcome and appreciation given him by his congregation.

Apparently the family and her friends kept bringing up the subject. "I wish people would leave me and Mr. Murray alone. How could anything so sudden and private get so widely spread? Some people are even calling to congratulate first Ellen and then me, confused as to which of us he proposed, much to our amusement. I wish they would never mention him again, because then I start to think about him, and I would much rather not. Some of his clerical friends invited him back to the Cape after a year for a conference, and I hear he refused, which puzzles them. Some declare that he will return, and they are sure he has not forgotten me. I hate to be made such a subject of discussion."

It seems that Andrew would not take no for an answer. He took the risk of writing her anyway. After Emma received a number of his cordial letters, she consented to continue a friendly correspondence with him. She admitted that her first letter was a cold answer to his very kind letter, and her parents expressed their wish that she had been kinder. Andrew asked forgiveness for the past and inquired whether he might entertain some hope for the future. Apparently the frequent correspondence got warmer with time.

Emma, however, continued to worry whether their characters were suitable to each other and determined that she would not make any final decision without further face-to-face acquaintance. "It is impossible by letters to find out whether or not there is really that lack of heart that initially troubled me, which would grate and mar every enjoyment," she wrote her sister.

Emma wrote that if Andrew wanted to take the risk of coming to see her again with the understanding that she was still uncertain about their relationship and reserved her right to decide, she just might be willing to see him again. However, Andrew must have been strongly persuasive in his many letters because by March of the following year he had convinced her through letters alone of his warm, true and faithful love, apparently with enough "romantic heart" that she consented to marry him even without waiting for another visit.

Suddenly Emma's mind was bombarded with the consequences of her new decision. It was her mother's turn to worry that her pretty, intelligent daughter was in danger of being swamped with domesticity in a wilderness parish far from home. She herself had left a comfortable home to come six thousand miles from "the civilization of England" to the uncertain, rustic life of South Africa. It was common knowledge that Bloemfontein boasted not more than a hundred one-story houses in the midst of widely-scattered farms. She worried that there was no law enforcement and little protection from raiders over the

Basutoland border. Furthermore, Emma would be expected to join the Dutch Church and learn to mix with some folk very strange to her city upbringing. Typical anxious mother!

Her mother's fears in turn caused Emma to doubt her own abilities and adjustment. "I know happiness depends more upon oneself than external circumstances, but I fear to undertake duties and responsibilities for which I might prove unequal. I could not be happy in rushing into new duties without some hope of performing them right. But still I trust God that He shall lead me to do what is right, and neither shrink from duties nor enter upon them thoughtlessly if they come."

Having made her decision, Emma began to speculate on her future and her position in relation to her prospective husband and his ministry.

> Mr. Murray works too hard and wears himself out. I only comfort myself that if I am not good enough or capable enough to be a spur to him, I can at least be a drag to keep him from overworking. I am not going to let him take those long preaching journeys alone. I shall go in the cart with him. [Was this the girl who didn't want to travel?] If I am with him he will be obliged to rest.
>
> The various congregations at the Cape try to persuade him to stay here, but I am glad God has called him to his present parish. I should not like him to become what is called a popular preacher. I think it much better to be a spiritual father to the poor and infant commonwealth, to help establish new, pioneer ministries, to take an interest and lead in the improvement of a young and rising population, than to be a town demagogue or oratory idol. When he was here at the Cape, I did not like it when old as well as young openly flattered him. I think he agreed and was glad to get away from it.

Emma would learn in years to come that the Lord calls to different fields at different times of their long lives. As the Lord of the Harvest, He would plant them sometimes in the fertile soil of the countryside and sometimes in needy urban areas, even overseas. And they would bring forth fruit from all fields to please Him.

Upon receiving Emma's letter at last declaring her love and accepting his proposal, Andrew hastily wrote that he would come soon.

Emma puzzled whether soon meant next month or next year. The journey by horse cart from Bloemfontein took at least three weeks, but Andrew, the impulsive, eager bridegroom-to-be traveled the distance in thirteen days. We are not told what condition the horses were in upon his arrival! He reached the Cape on May 31, ready to claim his bride—in haste again.

7

Covered Wagon Honeymoon

Once the young couple decided to marry, wedding plans had to be made in a hurry because Andrew felt it necessary to take his bride back to Bloemfontein as soon as possible. However, it happened to be a most inconvenient time for a wedding because Emma's father was not well, her mother was anxious about his health and worried about her son's departure to England. "Besides, how can we ever get Emma's traditional 'twelve dozen of everything' in the linens department of a bride's trousseau ready in time?"

"Never mind," pleaded Andrew impatiently, "the parsonage is fully stocked—and how can we possibly bring so many things with us by ox wagon?"

It was quickly accomplished, nevertheless, although the hemming of the table cloths and napkins was left for Emma to do later.

When Andrew observed the enormous quantity of "household necessities" for which he would have to arrange transportation, it gave him amused alarm. It was a given that Emma had to take her precious Singer sewing machine, an ungainly ancestor of the trim models of today. Emma had one of the first machines in Cape Town. That was nothing compared to his shock when Emma announced, "Of course I am taking my grand piano and other specially dear pieces of furniture and china!" Andrew probably had visions of the two of them trying to ford flooded streams and floating away on top of the piano, hugging pieces of English chinaware!

But his new bride and her family had their way. The expenses of the journey were tremendous, and it was a bad time of the year to travel both for themselves and for the transport animals because the season was quickly turning cold. The wagon was the largest obtainable, and the horses alone cost £140. But in the whirl of excitement the young couple did not regret it. It was all part of the fun of starting a new life together.

Andrew even made a profit on selling the wagon and animals when they reached home, a source of admiration to his new bride. "I think my husband, though he sometimes frightens others by his quick and bold way of doing things, always knows what he is about."

Emma's mother gave them one of their most valuable wedding presents by engaging an English servant, Mrs. Henly, to serve them at Bloemfontein. She proved a treasure with all her accomplishments, and took full charge of operational matters in the new Murray household to relieve her mistress.

The choice of a church for their wedding could have been a sensitive issue as the couple represented two distinct ecclesiastical poles—the Church of England and the Dutch Reformed Church. "Friendly discussions" were necessary but happy compromises made, with the ceremony taking place in the Dutch Reformed Church at Wynberg but conducted in English with Andrew's uncle, Rev. W. A. Stegmann, a minister of the Lutheran Church, officiating. The date was July 2, 1856. Andrew was twenty-eight and Emma twenty-one.

What did the ladies in the wedding party wear in mid-Victorian Cape Town, and what was the wedding like? Women readers want to know! One of the bridesmaids, Andrew's cousin Maggie, the fifteen-year-old daughter of the officiating minister, gave us a firsthand description:

> Uncle Andrew looked very handsome and his bride was beautiful. She wore plain white muslin flounced, and each of the flounces were ruched [pleated lace or net trimming at the collar and sleeves]. Her

hair was curled in front and she had a wreath and veil. There were four bridesmaids, two were sisters of Emma, a good friend, and myself. We all wore white dresses and white bonnets. Two of us wore pink silk mantles and the other two blue. There were two best men, one was Frederic, brother of the bride.

After the eleven o'clock ceremony, we drove to her parents' home where many friends were waiting to wish the couple joy. Then the family and a few friends sat down to a beautiful breakfast. Toasts were given and speeches made. When the wedding cake was cut, each of us bridesmaids got a little ornament from the top of it.

The bride went to change her dress, then she officially took leave of her parents, came out on the stoop, and we all said a short farewell. She had been cheerful all day, but I fancy she was most glad when that sad parting was past.

The new Mrs. Murray and her husband drove away down the lovely Feldhausen Oak Avenue, across the Flats to Stellenbosch, onto the first stage of their journey to her new home. This was to be the first of many journeys. In addition to traveling all over the country with her husband, Emma went to England and the Continent four or five times, once with five small children. She accompanied Andrew on one of his trips to the United States where they attended a conference in Chicago. This was the girl who didn't think she was up to travel!

Back to the honeymoon. Their wagon train consisted of a large mule wagon and a large covered wagon pulled by four horses. Their long journey lasted almost a month. Though an arduous trip, the beauty of some of the scenic places through which they passed helped to keep stars in the eyes of the young couple. They dined picnic fashion in the shadow of beautiful, lofty mountains, often by rolling streams foaming in bursting cascades. Sometimes they traveled until dark or even in the moonlight until ten o'clock.

Emma first heard her husband preach in Dutch on the Sundays en route when they stayed over at farm or village settlements. "One thing impressed me very much," wrote Emma to her family. "They often sing a hymn in the middle of the sermon to wake the people up! I thought it was time to leave, and prepared to do so, when they all sat down again and continued!"

After the two Sunday services on a particular occasion, the couple walked up the mountain "to enjoy its beauty and quiet and read and sing together until sunset, enjoying the grandeur and loneliness of the place."

As they progressed, the journey became much more difficult, but Emma was thrilled with the experience of camping out at night—she called it "real pioneering." Snow soon lay quite close on each side of the road as they traveled. "It was so cold," wrote Emma later, "that the only thing to do was to go to bed as soon as possible."

She registered delight at the different customs among the Dutch which she observed by traveling inland for the first time. "Oh, the multiplicity of children and the size of the babies! Ten or twelve children is the ordinary number. I wonder how it is that the Dutch have not swallowed up the land. I never saw such a marrying and children-loving people. Every youth of twenty is sure to be married. If you want to get to their hearts, just admire the babies or talk to the children. My husband is very good at both, he understands quieting a baby far better than I do, but then he has even now a little sister of six months and has always had some little brother or sister to play with."

Leaving the mountains behind, they came upon the wide, open, monotonous plains of the Karroo, without farms or houses. "When we halt at night, we speedily boil coffee while the animals are un-hitched and fed. The cart and wagon are fastened together. The cart was prepared by Mrs. Henly for our bedroom and is very snug and comfortable. The wagon is all lined with thick, green baize [soft, woolen fabric resembling felt]. Then out come cakes, bread, butter, milk, and cold meat and these are enjoyed as supper by the fireside in the bright moonlight. We often sing hymns, then have prayers and retire by the light of a carriage lamp. Getting up in the morning is the most difficult as my hands get numb with the cold.

"We were lost a few times and then rejoiced when we heard bleating of sheep or barking of dogs as indicative of some sheep farm where we could learn our direction. Once we lost some forage and goods off the wagon and had to send back three hours to search for it. The boy assigned to the task was followed by a wild dog and would have been eaten had not a second man on horseback overtaken him."

The wagon train detoured east so Andrew could introduce his bride to his family at Graaff-Reinet. They received a warm welcome and Emma was joyously accepted at once. She was amused at how the younger children adored her husband. Also, she observed, it was from his mother, to whom he was deeply attached, that he got his gaiety and feeling for colors, and scents, and pretty things.

Some insights into the character of Andrew help us understand his humanness and make us appreciate still more his deeply serious teachings and writings that rose from actual life experiences. It may surprise us to hear that some thought Andrew extravagant. His bride defended him against these remarks, considering him generous. "I don't feel anxious about that. I think it is more that other people are so close and stingy and can so little comprehend large views. If my husband must get a book, he gets a good one. He is fond of giving his sisters presents—dresses and shawls of the best quality."

The elder Rev. Murray openly expressed pride in his brilliant son even if he sometimes deplored his impulsiveness. He himself had married a girl half his age, sixteen, and never regretted it. Andrew's mother, Emma observed, was a quiet, gentle person much loved by all her children and a model wife and mother. "She makes all her husband's and children's clothes, superintends the cooking and baking, washing and candle making, yet looks after the lessons of the children. The youngest child is a baby of six months, a sweet little creature."

The next stop was Bloemfontein, Emma's new home for the next four eventful years.

8

"A New Idea of a Wife"

When the young couple finally arrived at Bloemfontein, instead of their coveted privacy they were besieged with visitors. In his bachelor days Andrew kept open house—anyone free to drop in at any time, and the pattern was never really broken.

Apparently they were hardly ever alone in the overcrowded house. Andrew's eldest sister stayed with them temporarily. Although not much older than Emma, she tried rather tactlessly to show her new sister-in-law how to run her house. Emma had very definite ideas about being her husband's *companion* rather than his *housekeeper*, intending to leave Mrs. Henly, her capable maid, to attend to routine matters. But sister-in-law problems were cheerfully compromised, and they became the best of friends for life.

Emma took upon herself the monumental task of establishing a healthy, uncluttered, unpressured home atmosphere so her husband could freely work for the Lord.

> To make an excitable, earnest spirit like my husband to rest, that is my most difficult duty and my greatest anxiety. People seem to think that a minister is public property and everyone's friend. From six a.m. until nine p.m. we are never sure of not having visitors. People have little sense of propriety. They walk in whether you are at breakfast or

dinner, and if at tea time, always expect to be offered at least a cup of coffee. The consumption of coffee is dreadful! Dutch people are so fond of it. People sit and talk with Andrew for hours. Andrew's opinion must be had about everything, and I can well understand how much he needed a wife and companion with the constant drain on him.

We have so little time to read. All day and night we just start to pick up a book and are interrupted. We have begun reading the *History of the Early Puritans, Neander's Church History, Brainerd's Life of Prayer,* and *The Earnest Student.* We try to read on certain evenings after we come back from Andrew's meetings or singing nights, but he is often too tired. After reading a quarter of an hour, his throat gets hoarse, and then he likes to lie down and have me sing to him.

Our delightful gardening is a diversion in the fresh air and does help Andrew rest besides providing so many delicious vegetables and beautiful flowers and fruit harvests.

Concerning Andrew's health, I am sorry to say he is more tired and unwell than I have seen him so far during our married life. So many services on weekends with constant company in the home quite knocks him down. Also the standing around with the many details of all that goes on in the parish with no place in the vestry for him to rest. I am trying to devise all sorts of plans to get a sofa there, for this fatigue will not do. It is strange that he is something like me in that his fatigue always exhibits itself in excitement and restlessness, then it is followed by complete exhaustion. This morning he seems more dead than alive.

But don't fancy that because of his weakness he is an old shriveled-looking thing! Andrew is remarkably young and fresh looking and exhibits no *outward* signs of weakness. He never knew a day's illness until he overexerted himself in his holy duties in the wilderness. His constitution is good, only overused, and his wife does her best to prevent that now, with the help of God.

Commenting on Andrew's preaching: "His weekday English services are mainly for the young. I am obliged to listen very attentively to all his sermons for he makes me his critic and always expects to know just what I think. I tell him it is good for him that he has a simple congregation for whom he must bring his ideas to their comprehension. He is obliged to clip his wings or else, I think we would be in some danger if he had a clever and intellectual congregation. He would become too fanciful or too new, if I may use this expression, in his sermons. Now they must be plain and practical, and shorn of the new, varied, and perhaps a little wild interpretations and symbolic meanings that he favors *me* with."

An insight into the close relationship of Andrew and his wife is reflected in her frank recital to her family:

> I am anxious to be a good housekeeper. But Andrew *never* finds fault with anything I do, and I am afraid I don't understand yet about being economical, though he never says I am extravagant or even hints things might be better. Sometimes I wish he would say so because I know so little. He always listens to my smallest household trouble even with such serious spiritual things on his mind and tries to find me a remedy. He does everything I ask him and gets me whatever I wish. You cannot imagine a more sympathizing, loving husband, so tender and gentle to his little wife.
>
> Yet he seems made to command, a sort of bishop or benevolent little pope among his people. I tell him that I sometimes feel afraid when he is talking to other people, but never for myself. He had so early in life been accustomed to responsibility and command and to act decisively for himself and others that it has imparted a great amount of decision and strength to his character.
>
> Ah, but you will think I am always praising my husband. I only wish you knew him, I feel sure you would love him. I certainly never knew before that I could be so bound to anyone or love anyone so much. It seems a new faculty I was perfectly unconscious of before, almost overwhelming me in its strength and depth of joy.
>
> The only tinge of sadness I have, though I would not wish it otherwise, is that his deep earnestness and feeling for the matters of God so often exhaust his physical strength and remind me that he is human and life is uncertain. Yet I know that "man is immortal till his work is done," and I pray he may be long spared to be useful in his day and generation.

Emma's prayer was answered in the long life and wide influence for Christ with which God honored Andrew in spite of his lifetime "thorn in the flesh"—physical weakness—which threw him totally on the strength of the Lord.

Emma had no intention of drifting into the traditional pattern of a tame, domestic wife. Andrew's work necessitated his absence for three or four days every two weeks, and she was a capable helper to look after all his affairs. She did considerable parish visiting in the village and taught in a school for colored people three times a week. (The term "colored" in South African terminology at that time referred to people who were of mixed racial descent.) Emma was also responsible for a regular "book evening" when people came to buy hymn books, Bibles and other books, handled the accounts for various matters, helped answer the mountains of correspondence as her husband's secretary, filed his papers and books, was organist of the church, and taught in the Sunday School.

One of their guests was a clergyman from Holland. During the course of conversation with Andrew about his sermon preparation, Andrew called to his wife matter-of-factly, "Dear, where did that idea in last Sunday's sermon come from?"

Emma promptly replied, "From chapter five of Brainerd's biography." She was known for always being able to trace the sources of Andrew's ideas to the many books they read together.

"Ha!" said the amazed Hollander, "She must be *the new idea of a wife*." The traditional Dutch idea was that the wife was primarily a mother and housekeeper. He added, "Having a living encyclopedia for a wife must be a useful possession!"

Emma, with a young bride's naiveté and perhaps a tinge of pride felt that she, as a companion-wife, contrasted favorably with "other clergymen's and missionaries' wives who are so entirely taken up with household cares as to be quite unable to exert themselves in aiding their husband's labors or in interesting themselves in the parish work, which they may totally neglect." She zealously guarded certain quiet hours for reading and talking with her husband. "When Andrew is tired, he is refreshed by a little talk or music or walk with me, without always being in danger of interruption by a servant or guest."

If Emma thought she was overwhelmed by her responsibilities at *that* time, it was nothing compared to their added duties and ministry when the Murrays undertook supervision as rector and wife of the newly established Grey College in Bloemfontein. The College was founded in 1856 by others for the instruction of youth and the training of men for the teaching profession. It was formally opened in 1859 with a Dutch teacher, an English teacher, but no headmaster. As the rector, Andrew assumed that position. His duties included general administration and management of the boarding department. The latter involved Emma in a significant way. To her new household she added an "extended family" of several dozen boy boarders, ages nine to eighteen, plus twenty "day boys." She became a very young surrogate "Mama" on duty day and night, in their sickness as well as in their health.

For Andrew this was a challenge of a different sort. He wrote, "Religious education must, I think, become the watchword of our church before we can expect abiding fruit from our labors. . . ." Apparently his brother John wrote that he hoped Andrew would soon be relieved of school duties.

He replied, "I hardly wish it. I feel deeply interested in the work and do not think it will be too much for me as long as I have no direct instruction to give. It is an experiment to see what influence can be exerted upon the boys by much prayer and close, daily contacts with them. Will the result be more encouraging than preaching? Pray for me that the spirit of faith and love may possess me, that wisdom and diligence may be given me from on high for the work. Our number today is fourteen with the prospect of four more soon."

Meal planning and the purchase of supplies nearly overwhelmed Emma at times. Perhaps overdramatizing it a little for her Cape family's sympathy, she wrote:

> Fancy me as the head of such a large establishment! But sometimes I can't bear puzzling my brain trying to turn a tough, sinewy piece of dry-looking wildebeest into a savory soup or stew and then to find, after all, I have not succeeded. Then I am told that [the village women] manage so much better! Or to calculate the expense saved by baking dripping biscuits, since coffee and butter are scarce in winter. Or trying to cut up a dozen, large cabbage heads for sauerkraut or pickling for winter store. Or to make vinegar from old sugar bags when we are done with them, or to dry fruit, or to kill one's own sheep and save the fat for candles and certain other parts for soap. Or to sigh over shopping

accounts which run up most unexpectedly, work and scrimp as you will. Or to try looking like a lady on as small expense as possible, and then have someone suspect that we live luxuriously.

My dear Andrew has both a fault and virtue rolled into one. He has too generous a heart and gives to the utmost farthing whenever some unfortunate comes by. Often he unexpectedly invites some quantity of people home to eat or sleep, apologizing, "I don't know what you'll say, dear wife, but I could not help it." There are no inns in these villages, and every traveler thinks he has a claim on a minister's hospitality. Of course I make the best of it, so we have put up beds everywhere, and it seems I am always making beds. I give out stores to the needy without a sigh, and somehow we manage without suffering any personal inconvenience. Nor getting into debt, I hope.

We must just do right and trust God and not peer into the future, or it would seem an impossibility to bring up a large extended family in this way. I know far more about economizing now than at first and can make do with less. God is helping me not to feel too anxious.

But life was not all scrimping and saving, and Emma ends her letter happily talking about music and books. A Major Fraser visited them bringing some beautiful music with him, "all the best songs from recent operas, *La Traviata* and *Il Trovatore*, besides other really good German music. He sings and tuned my piano and has quite set me to practicing again. I love to sketch as often as I can, and intend to mail you a sketch of our house and grounds. Thank you for the promise of new books you are sending. A new book quickens me so, and Andrew and I have something delightful to share together."

Andrew's love for young people and desire to influence them spiritually made him a natural for the rector's position. The Murrays moved into new school buildings not far from the parsonage. They ate all their meals with the boys, and Andrew thoroughly enjoyed conducting prayers morning and evening.

Emma coped well with the challenge of twenty-five boys plus her husband and later her own babies with only one recurring regret: "My poor brain is usually so engrossed with the business of the ministry and whirl of domestic life and child care that I am almost unfit for reading and intellectual enjoyment! Lately I prefer the piano or fancy work and can finally understand how people much accustomed to drudgery gravitate to such things to maintain a sane mind."

However, because she was so literary minded, she encouraged Andrew in that direction to his great benefit—also to ours as readers of his books in later generations, books which would have worldwide influence for God's Kingdom in years to come. Because of Emma's unflagging enthusiasm and drive, Andrew got down to the task of providing suitable reading material for his people by writing it himself. Andrew had just received a first copy of his first book, the *Life of Christ for Children*, written in Dutch. His brother John was already into book writing and publishing.

In fact, Emma may have been a little jealous for Andrew's sake of John's success in that venture. John's first two books were selling extremely well, and she did not see why her husband, whom she considered far more brilliant, should be left behind. "I tell Andrew that his brother possesses no shining talents or public eloquence to make him so popular, but he is the more diligent in *business*, the most fervent in *spirit*."

She reflected, "I like this book writing very much, when we can find time for it, for I am my husband's amanuensis [secretary]. We are doing another book now in Dutch after publishing the first one for children." This was in 1858 when Andrew was thirty years old. "It is selling well and should pay its own expenses soon. In perhaps eighteen months there may be a little profit, enough to invest in doing our next publication. John has been very much blessed in his publications, some of which are extensively circulated and have gone through several editions. Cautious, quiet Scotsman that he is, he has always made his books pay for themselves. What he loses on one, he is sure to gain on another!"

9

The Nest God Intended

Emma continued to share the details of her new, adventurous life with her Cape Town family and her sister in India with a continual stream of letters. No incident was too small to share, no impression or thought too private to write about.

Apparently it was the custom of the times for the couple to sign a "prenuptial" contract of sorts they called "The Agreement." Emma's mother made sure Emma's father supervised the drafting of it and would put into writing that Andrew's wife should always be provided with at least two servants. Mrs. Henly was one, and the other turned out to be a wild, little Kaffir boy about twelve. (Kaffir is what black people were called in those days.) He had never been trained for serving but was quick to learn. Emma taught him to set the table and brush his master's clothes. "I named my very dirty, ragged little fellow Cupid," Emma wrote. His escapades made good stories for Emma to write about.

On one occasion Mrs. Henly, who was very fastidious and orderly, lost her temper with the laziness and lack of obedience of Cupid. She did not speak the Dutch language and was unwilling to learn it, but thought that if she yelled loud enough in English, others would understand. Cupid resented being shouted at.

Emma wrote, "They had a misunderstanding of language. Mrs. Henly got angry and chased Cupid from the kitchen. Now Cupid is really the son of a chief with royal blood in his veins, and he was highly insulted. He sulked and refused to mind her, nor carry out his duties. The Kaffirs have a great sense of their own dignity. I am vexed with her and told her she must not offend him by halloaing [their term] at him at the top of her voice. I think the boy is trainable and useful and I don't want to lose him."

Evidently Mrs. Henly and Cupid ironed out their differences and a few weeks later he invited her and the Murrays' coachman to visit his father's Kraal (native village surrounded by a stockade). Mrs. Henly was impressed by the clean huts and saw that Cupid's father indeed held a high position and owned herds of sheep. A good time was had by all.

Emma, however, found Dutch housekeeping quite untidy and "dirty beyond belief" compared to her middle class urban standard. As a bachelor who traveled much, Andrew paid little attention to domestic matters, leaving it to unsupervised servants. Emma assumed her new role by having all the wallpaper washed because the original pattern was hardly visible. The parsonage, like most of the houses in the village, had a thatched roof and mud floors instead of flooring boards because of the absence of local timber. Emma soon discovered how those mud floors were to be kept.

> The surface is smeared periodically with cattle dung applied with the palm of the hand in a circular movement. This gives the floor a lovely polish and color, though the smell is overpowering at first. The next day the odor is not so bad, and I am told such floors keep the house beautifully warm in these bitter, Free State winters.
>
> You asked about carpets, Mama? We lay them over the mud floors and apart from sprinkling a little water over the floor before sweeping each day, no more care is needed. The church has promised to build on two more rooms for us which we badly need.
>
> A stream issuing from a spring flows by our large property. We collect watercress from it which we often have for dinner. Cupid fetches all the water for our use from the well in the village, using an old hand pump with a wooden roller and yards of rope to which a bucket is attached.

Mama, you would love our large garden which is surrounded with a high stone wall with trailing vines. It is planted with a great variety of vegetables and fruit trees. Andrew and I both love to garden and we have already sown the seeds we brought from the Cape. When we suspect a frost may come, we lay some branches over the new seed beds and cover them with skins overnight.

Emma's acquired satisfaction with her unusual floor covering was soon to be tested. The Western Cape has a Mediterranean climate with winter rain and hardly a storm. But the Murrays' parish was in a rainfall region with violent storms of frightening thunder and lightning. The Murrays often experienced storms while traveling by cart, describing the lightning as darting in and out of the wagon and pursuing them relentlessly.

Emma wrote her mother about a violent mid-November thunderstorm. She and Andrew took pride in their cultivated garden, especially the flower beds with an abundance of roses, dahlias, sweet williams and some rare blossoms from their imported bulbs, and were happy to share it with their guests. On that occasion their visitors stayed late through afternoon tea enjoying the garden.

> By evening the air became oppressive and sultry. That night just past midnight came a storm such as I never witnessed before. Even with my mouth close to Andrew's ear I had to shout to be heard. Lightning seemed to glare right through the blankets and pillows. Then came hailstones nearly the size of plums, battering against the roof till I thought it must surely break through. The thunder rolled directly over our heads.
>
> After more than an hour it let up, and by the lightning flashes we could see that hail lay a foot thick in the garden. We beheld a miserable wreck. Our precious flowers and plants were torn to shreds, and apples, plums and peaches were strewn over the ground. All our lettuce and spinach was beaten down to nothing, everything stripped, vines torn down, bunches of grapes scattered over the ground. A melancholy spectacle!
>
> Because the hail plugged up the downspouts on the roof, the water backed up and rose to a foot high against the new door just framed between our dining room and the kitchen. It soon broke into the

room and everything was flooded, rushing into other rooms as well. The carpets and everything else were soaked. Andrew in his nightshirt was trying to raise my piano up on boards. The servants bailed out the water with tin dishes. Andrew would not allow me to get up out of bed, but everyone else was busy. Mrs. Henley was making coffee and boiling water. They did not finish until four o'clock. I was very frightened as I lay alone in the only dry room in the house with the lightning glaring with a lurid light on the white hail outside and the thunder rolling overhead. It became suddenly very cold and the wind whistled in everywhere.

You can imagine what the flood did to the mud floors. I had to go about in galoshes over plank bridges. We were forced to move temporarily to a little house of two rooms within five minutes of the parsonage. For days we were busy sorting everything that was damp and drying and saving what we could. Now Andrew is finally determined to have our floors boarded no matter what the cost. Andrew says God will make the garden revive again and the fruit trees will bud once more.

Secretly Andrew had feared his wife might not do well in the household management department because she was thought to be "literary." He had made up his mind to endure any domestic shortcomings because he loved her, and she had so many other endearing qualities. He was pleasantly surprised to see that everything looked cleaner and brighter than ever before. Andrew was genuinely vocal with his praise of Emma's neat housekeeping and management of the household staff, all the accounts and her capable hospitality.

Getting more closely acquainted with the village folk and Andrew's congregation was a greater challenge for Emma. She found it a weariness to constantly talk to people whose ideas were limited and with whom conversation was a constant repetition. She discovered that the people were pleased when she looked happy and content and when she praised the little village and made attempts to talk with them. They, in turn, had been afraid that Andrew's English wife would be too high class for them and dissatisfied, so she would try to persuade Andrew to leave. Emma had visions of uplifting their thoughts and tastes beyond everyday affairs, perhaps by entertaining at a monthly tea party, but she couldn't find topics to interest them.

She tried to break the ice with the closest neighbor children, of whom there were dozens, by inviting them over to see her new pet, a little springbok (miniature gazelle) she fed out of a bottle with a sponge at the top. She added a crane and guinea fowl to her little zoo. Sometimes when she went walking, all of them would follow her, much to the delight of the townspeople.

"Emma is happy and I am happy," Andrew wrote to his brother John. "She is beginning to get on well with the Dutch people in spite of her deficient language. She is very eager to be useful, but sometimes I am at a loss to suggest how!"

Yes, Emma was happy, and repeated it often in her letters. "Andrew possesses the highest and best qualities above all men and is free from all their faults. I have never known such overflowing happiness in my life hitherto, and joy beyond my expectations and our deserts. We both feel this. It is far greater than our warmest feelings ever anticipated. It is strange what perfect harmony and suitability there is between us in our characters. But you will think me foolish for talking thus, and Ellen and Lucy will laugh when they recall how I worried that Andrew did not have a warm, affectionate heart."

Emma did travel with Andrew as often as possible, sharing the simple accommodations the farm people provided for him and satisfied to partake of their coarse food. She soon learned that it was advisable to take plenty of their own "survival food" along, especially extras like cake and raisins and fruit. On one trip Emma was exposed to the Doppers, a very strict religious sect living on farms. They were suspicious of any modern innovations. She described their overnight stay with a Dopper family.

> These people are sort of Quakers and the women always wear hoods or bonnet-like coverings even indoors. Their dress is primitive. The men never wear suspenders nor do the women put stays [flat strips used for stiffening corsets or other apparel] in their dresses. They speak in a drawling manner with a nasal twang, are slow in their movements and have a peculiar way of sitting. Unlike the Quakers, they are dirty and untidy. The bad weather drove us to seek shelter with them. Another minister arrived at the same time to seek shelter.

Fortunately, I always carry sheets and our sheepskin blanket because we were all assigned to sleep in the same large room where there were three beds with only curtains between. The old man and his wife tumbled into one, Mr. Roux and another sojourner into another, and we had the third. I contrived to smuggle my clean sheets and blanket behind the curtain and quickly made our bed right on top of the one destined for us—which evidently many had occupied before our turn came. Besides this, there were four children sleeping around on the floor.

Emma continued her travels with Andrew even during her pregnancy. She wrote home, "My darling Mama, I find my new life so exciting it is difficult to keep a quiet mind. Sometimes I don't know whether I am crying or laughing for joy or sadness. My husband laughs at me, calling me a regular April day because I laugh and cry all in one moment. I am so well but really worrying about getting too stout and losing my figure. It is astonishing how I can jolt about over rough roads and through rivers from six in the morning till six at night and often not feel as tired as I do at home."

She had written to a friend, "Don't be too surprised when I tell you I intend to present Andrew with a little temptation and interruption to his studies in the shape of a little son or daughter next April, if all is well. . . . I cannot yet realize the idea of myself being a mother!" Emma did not consider herself the maternal type by nature and must have suspected that her wings would be clipped when she had a small child running about. Finding her new life far too interesting, we are not surprised that she did not go into any kind of retirement while waiting for the baby.

There was no adequately skilled medical or nursing help available. When the time came for the birth of their first baby, Emma did not seem to have been very worried about herself. Her local doctor was not very qualified, having come to the South African countryside as a missionary with little medical knowledge. But he soon had plenty of experience in maternity cases in the Free State. Mrs. Henly was a most capable nurse. Nursing care was looked upon as part of the normal work of the ladies of the family.

Emma's mother sent lovely baby clothes but did not volunteer to come and help with the infant. She wrote, "I pray God to give you a safe and comfortable childbearing and make you the rejoicing parents of a living, healthy babe. My trust and confidence are in Him to do all things well for you. I was never a very good attendant in sickness, and do believe that I even create more distress on such occasions."

On the twentieth of April the Murrays' firstborn was delivered. Andrew wrote to his brother John, "I send you glad tidings. God has been very kind. Emma suffered but little, and the sweet babe and mother are doing well."

After their first child, a daughter, was born, Emma's life did indeed change. Now she began to understand and sympathize with what other ministers' wives with children really *did* have to contend with. "A great difficulty with me is not the lack of time, but its management. I cannot write or keep any account of time or study Dutch or count upon *any* peace. Little Emmie, as her Papa calls her, wakes, needs constant attention, people come, duties press, baby needs me again, and time flies. . . ." Ah, Emma was learning!

A second baby girl soon joined the Murray family. Little Mary provided company for Little Emmie, but of course doubled the work for Mama, and before long doubled the mischief two little girls could get into.

Emma took motherhood in her stride, and simply added it to her many other responsibilities. Emma was a clerk to her husband, keeping his important documents, letters, accounts, and dispensing household money for purchasing. She also kept records of church funds and book sales money. "Sometimes I hear 'Darling, darling!' every ten minutes, especially on post days and when visitors arrive. I must always be ready to attend to his wants. But that is my joy. Andrew's correspondence is enormous and because of the weakness in his hands from his early illness, he dictates to me and I write the messages."

She was also organist in Andrew's church. She played a small organ without pipes where the bellows were worked by pedals with the feet.

Dutch church music is rather complicated. At the end of each line are short interludes which I have to play nicely to introduce the next line. The time and chords are often difficult. I have to keep pumping gently with my feet to keep the bellows constantly filling. Mama, you would be amused. I so enjoy the Dutch singing, the hymns and psalms are exceedingly beautiful and simple and the people sing so heartily. They have an instinctive love for and taste for music, though they lack cultivation.

Between ourselves, Mama, I think the Dutch church services are too long, three hours in the morning, two in the afternoon, and the whole fatigue resting on the minister. Villagers and farmers come from a distance sometimes once a month or fortnightly, living in a tent or wagon. Because they want to use their trip to the fullest they would even like to begin church services at daybreak. So now we have opened a Sunday School and many are eager to attend.

We have ordered dealwood, ready-made seats from Cape Town, but they are long in arriving. Presently people carry their chairs in, often on their backs. Nor is the ceiling finished. Sometimes swallows and occasionally owls whirl over our heads while my husband is trying to preach and maintain reverence. But the people are very attentive when Andrew preaches.

During at least three winter months our church building is so cold and drafty that it is all but unbearable to aged persons and invalids. Some of the congregation wear white nightcaps with tassels. It is common to have mothers with crying babies and small children wandering in and out and creating a disturbance. Sometimes Andrew has to stop his sermon and urge the mothers to sit with their children near the doors.

Ah, but again I must say that happy as I was at home and much as I love it still, I am even happier now than I ever have been. It seems to me that I have found the nest for which God intended me. I serve God with plenty of the work I had always wished for, and for which He suited me. We have a nice little parsonage, the difficulties so many have to contend with made smooth for me, the loving heart and intellectual companionship of my husband, happy, healthy children, and a sense of being a comfort and help to others. I have full scope for all my energies of mind, body and heart, so that I never had such an expanded spirit.

Because there was no tailor in the village, Emma was kept busy with her treadle Singer sewing machine. She asked for special white grass cloth to be sent from the Cape and made Andrew some cool, traveling hip jackets. She even tried her hand at sewing him a pair of white trousers. "I thought it well to learn. I did not venture to cut them out by myself, but watched Mrs. Henly." Emma made her own dresses and their little children's dresses as well. "There is so much to do that I often don't have a minute to myself from six-thirty in the morning till eight or past at night."

Nor was there a barber in Bloemfontein. Married men had their wives cut their hair, and mothers cut the hair of their children. Emma learned to do the same for Andrew. "A certain unruly, thick shock of his hair is always a trial to me. Crop it as I will, there is no thinning or control of it. Fortunately it is not red, but of a rich brown with a golden curl or wave just in front. In a lady it would be a beauty!"

The last four years of Andrew's ministry at Bloemfontein were happily different from his previous ones as a bachelor. His health eventually improved, although he was still far from robust. His duties as rector of Grey College were not too heavy, but they kept him from wandering too far from his own parish and newly established home. When he did travel, Emma often went with him, even with little children in tow. With Emma managing their home and sheltering him from overwork, Andrew had much more time for study and writing.

10

Revival at Last

Barely thirty years old, Andrew had a wide reputation as a young minister of exceptional abilities, earnestness, and intensity of purpose. Invitations to new pulpits were frequent and repeated, each to larger areas of influence and more cultured people than the pioneers beyond the Orange River among whom he spent his most active years. He continued to refuse, until in 1860 he believed one to be the call of God. It was to Worcester, an important educational center.

This growing township was about a hundred miles east of Cape Town, comparatively accessible, and seemed to need the kind of energetic spiritual guidance for which Andrew was gifted. The emotional ordeal of severing from his pioneer pastorate of eleven years was traumatic, but Andrew was convinced God had ordained he should move on.

In retrospect, although Andrew reproached himself continually for not having been as faithful and fruitful in the lives of his people as he wished, he gave himself totally to them, and the results which flowed from his ministry were in every way remarkable. Throughout his life and afterward, men and women recounted how it was during the early ministry of "young Mr. Murray" that they were converted or they more fully consecrated themselves to their Lord through his powerful public preaching and earnest individual exhortations.

His daughter later wrote, "The photographs taken of father at that young age represent him as a stern-looking man, and my mother often spoke of his hard criticisms of and deep dissatisfaction with himself. He would say: 'My work seems vain, the people have no real consciousness of sin, no real dread of it; there is so much frivolity and lightheartedness as they come so thoughtlessly before God and to His Table, with no real preparation and no heart-searching.' He was constantly probing his own heart and blaming himself for the lack of consecration in his hearers."

But God was leading His servant on and opening before him through his own experiences the secret of a life of victory and peace into which he was to lead many who would never meet him. God was fitting him for a worldwide ministry.

Andrew became as deeply burdened for revival as his father had been—as much for himself as for his people. Outwardly he had intense zeal, and the word "earnestness" occurs over and over in descriptions of him. For this he was admired and praised, and at this very point he was the most introspective and disappointed because he viewed himself far short of God's power.

"My own work loses much of the value it once possessed even in my own eyes. Somehow I have not yet been able to employ my Lord's strength instead of my own. My prayer for a revival, in which I have become somewhat careless, is held back by the increasing sense of *my* unfitness for the holy work of the Spirit's ministry."

Again he referred to "that awful pride and self-complacency which have hitherto ruled in my heart." It was that experience and later insights and victory through it that gave rise to his famous book titled *Humility*. It was because Andrew himself had such a battle with pride. "Nothing but a crucified Jesus revealed in the soul can give a humble spirit."

Even as God was searching his heart and pointing out pride, Andrew seemed to have the unconscious inner attitude that it *had to be preaching* that would bring forth revival—that it would depend on what *man* did, even on what *he* did. It is significant that when revival came, it was described as "not as a rule the direct result of the preaching of God's Word" by any particular person, including Andrew!

In fact, when the deep work of the Spirit broke forth among his people, not only did Andrew not initiate it or even recognize it, but he opposed it and tried his best to *stop* it. Was it because *he* did not have control of it? In any case, God was in the process of answering his prayers for humility!

God had been breaking up the fallow ground for the outpouring of His Spirit in South Africa for many years. It was all a part of the larger outpouring taking place simultaneously in America and Europe. Not only had Rev. Andrew Murray, Sr., devoted every Friday evening to prayer for revival, but later other similarly burdened ministers united with him in prayer. They prayed consistently for *thirty* years and waited in faith; then the glorious answer came.

Even at Worcester, Andrew's new pastorate, God raised up a group of revival intercessors who for many years had worn a footpath to a hilltop overlooking the village so they might better pray for the people. The minister who preceded Andrew intensely prayed and worked for revival.

Andrew's induction to this new charge coincided with the first of many significant conferences arranged by the newly opened Theological Seminary of Stellenbosch, to which ministers and elders came from every area. On the agenda were both missions and revival. God was about to do something with His mighty power on both these issues which the godly men, sincere as they were, thought they somehow could manage.

Concerning personnel for missions, ministers for the pulpits, and Christian teachers, the situation was critical. There were twenty-six ministerial vacancies in the Dutch Reformed Church of South Africa.

Andrew gave a moving address: "Where are we to find assistance? Can we devise no plan by which to supply the need? In vain have we written to France, Germany, Switzerland, and America for assistance in carrying out our mission project: no men can be found. . . . How are we to do it unless *we* can find men for the work? . . . It is for these reasons that we think it necessary to commission someone to visit Holland and to bring back a number of ministers and missionaries."

The resolution was passed with enthusiasm and a committee appointed to launch it. Passage and expense money needed to be raised for the delegate, and the enterprise drew widespread attention. Andrew found himself subsequently busy issuing appeals to the churches, visiting congregations, addressing gatherings and stimulating general interest and support. As it turned out, the recruitment was successful in that eleven ministers responded, two designated for the mission field, plus two school principals, two teachers, and four church helpers. However, much human zeal, time and money were expended to barely scratch the surface of the need.

Looking at it from the vantage point of what God was about to do among His needy people, one of the fruits of the forthcoming revival in the single congregation of Worcester was that "*fifty* young men offered themselves for the ministry of the Word, when previously it was almost impossible to find men for the work." God undoubtedly has ways and means by His supernatural power to accomplish all His works, fully supply all needs of personnel and finances, and the power for the tasks, which are beyond our human devisings and zeal—*if* we wait on Him for *His* ways.

What Andrew learned through this experience and his part in the coming revival permeates all of his subsequent teachings and writings in such books as *The Spirit of Christ*, *The Key to the Missionary Problem*, and *The Full Blessing of Pentecost*.

Exactly how did revival start in South Africa? We will trace the thread of these important events with verbatim quotes from eyewitnesses. Andrew's induction to the Worcester pastorate took place on Whitsunday (Pentecost) during the previously mentioned conference. Andrew delivered his inaugural sermon from 2 Corinthians 3:8, "How shall not the ministration of the Spirit be rather glorious?"

Great numbers of people from outside the congregation attended that worship service in addition to all the key delegates from Dutch Reformed churches throughout South Africa. Great expectations were aroused that the Lord would richly bless the ministry of Andrew in that place. God was preparing through that united touch upon His people gathered there not only the Worcester congregation but scattered parishes throughout the country for the remarkable manifestations of the power and quickening influence of His Holy Spirit coming very soon.

A paper which traced the fresh visitations of the Spirit on His Church in history was presented at the Worcester conference. The speaker then asked, "Is not such a revival equally necessary in South Africa?" He followed by stating the conditions upon which God could be expected to revive His work in the midst of the years. Earnest discussion followed. Another speaker told about the rise and progress of the recent revival in America, and of the circumstances which fostered its growth and spread. These addresses made a deep impression on those attending the conference. Individual members carried back to their homes a new sense of responsibility and hushed expectation that God *would indeed* lovingly visit His people with fresh outpourings of His grace.

The actual beginnings were very quiet without any of the special means thought necessary to kindle the flame of spiritual life. Most of the congregations represented at the conference were those in which the awakening of religious fervor appeared the earliest. This was seen initially in increased attendance at prayer meetings, with many new prayer circles established. The congregations of Montagu and Worcester were first touched. It was amazing that the awakening was not confined to the towns and villages but felt in totally isolated places without outside contacts, even on remote farms where men and women were suddenly seized with emotions to which they had been utter strangers a few weeks or even a few days before.

For example, a weekly prayer meeting had been attempted in one of the sections of the Worcester congregation some months before, but so little interest was generated that the attendance remained at three or four. But when God began to move in 1860, young and old, parents and children, without distinction of color, flocked to that prayer meeting, driven by a common impulse to cast themselves before God and utter their cries of repentance. In places where prayer meetings were unknown a year before, the people now complained because meetings ended an hour too soon! Not only weekly but daily prayer meetings were demanded by the people, even three times a day—and even among children.

Still some doubted that this was a work of God. They had prayed for years for revival but did not recognize God's answer. Strange scenes were witnessed with this rising tide of blessing. Primary sources do not describe the details but comment that "an outsider, unacquainted with the workings of the Spirit of God, would have called them undiluted fanaticism." Yet the Lord graciously kept His people from serious excesses.

This quote from an eyewitness, Rev. J. C. deVries, gives us a clearer picture of what happened at Worcester.

> On a certain Sunday evening there were gathered in a little hall some sixty young people. I was leader of the meeting, which began with a hymn and a lesson from God's Word, after which I prayed. Three or four others gave out a verse of a hymn and prayed, as was the custom. Then a colored girl of about fifteen years of age, in service with a nearby farmer, rose at the back of the hall and asked if she too might propose a hymn. At first I hesitated, not knowing what the meeting would think, but better thoughts prevailed, and I replied, Yes. She gave out her hymn verse and prayed in moving tones.
>
> While she was praying, we heard, as it were, a sound in the distance, which came nearer and nearer, until the hall seemed to be shaken; with one or two exceptions, the whole meeting began to pray, the majority in audible voice, but some in whispers. Nevertheless, the noise made by the concourse was deafening.
>
> A feeling which I cannot describe took possession of me. Even now, 43 years after these occurrences, the events of that never-to-be-forgotten night pass before my mind's eye like a soul-stirring panorama. I feel again as I then felt, and I cannot refrain from pushing my chair backwards, and thanking the Lord fervently for His mighty deeds.

While that meeting was going on, it seems that Andrew was preaching in English elsewhere in the church building. He was not present during the beginning of the events. When his service was over, an elder passing the door of the hall heard the noise, peeped in, and ran to call Andrew who returned with him at a run. Our eyewitness continues:

> Mr. Murray came forward to the table where I knelt praying, touched me, and made me understand that he wanted me to rise.

He then asked me what had happened. I related everything to him. Then he walked down the room for some distance and called out as loudly as he could, "People, silence!" But the praying continued. In the meantime, I kneeled down again. It seemed to me that if the Lord was coming to bless us, I should not be upon my feet but on my knees.

Mr. Murray then called loudly again, "People, I am your minister sent from God! Silence!" But there was no stopping the noise. No one heard him, but all continued praying and calling on God for mercy and pardon.

Mr. Murray then returned to me and told me to start the hymn-verse commencing "Help de ziel die raadloos shreit" ("Aid the soul that helpless cries"). I did so. But the emotions were not quieted and the meeting went right on praying. Mr. Murray then prepared to depart, saying, "God is a God of order, and here everything is confusion!" With that he left the hall.

We may wonder at Andrew's attitudes and actions upon that occasion. He had longed and prayed for revival for so many years, and had heard detailed reports about how God was manifesting Himself by His Spirit in other countries in the same manner as He had on many occasions in history. How was it then that he tried to interrupt, even stop the work of the Spirit? Although the Dutch Church was known for its calm, unemotional approach to religion, it was *just that* which Andrew deplored, and which, by his own intense zeal and fiery preaching, he was seeking to break through. Could it have been that his ego was wounded because the moving of the Spirit wasn't happening *as a result of his own preaching*? In fact, that he had not been present to guide it?

It would not do to speculate why Andrew called upon his own authority as their minister sent from God to stop a group in earnest prayer. Moreover, these were young people who were traditionally respectful and obedient to their elders, especially to their ecclesiastical head. We only conjecture, but from this episode we may nevertheless take our own lessons.

Prayer meetings were held every evening after that. It seems the pattern was the same each time, although no one set it. At the beginning of the meeting there was generally great silence; no one made efforts to stir up emotions, but after the second or third prayer the whole hall would be moved as before, with no human prompting. Everyone would begin to pray aloud.

This was certainly *not* the custom of the Dutch Reformed churches at that time, nor did anyone teach them to do so. Sometimes the gathering would continue until three in the morning. Even then, many wished to stay longer. As the people returned to their homes in the middle of the night they went singing joyously through the streets. The number of people participating so increased that the prayer meeting had to be moved to the school building, and that soon overflowed. Hundreds of farmers from the country streamed into the village to join the meetings.

On the first Saturday evening in the larger meeting house, Andrew was the leader. Our eyewitness continues:

> Mr. Murray read a portion of Scripture, made a few observations on it, engaged in prayer, and then gave others the opportunity to pray. During the prayer which followed his, we heard again the same sound in the distance. It drew nearer and nearer and on a sudden the whole gathering was praying.
>
> That evening a stranger had been standing at the door from the beginning of the meeting, watching the proceedings. Mr. Murray descended from the platform and again moved up and down among the people, trying to quiet them. The stranger tiptoed forward from the door, touched the thirty-two year old clergyman gently, and said in English, "I think you are the minister of this congregation. Be careful what you do, for it is the Spirit of God that is at work here. I have just come from America, and this is precisely what I witnessed there."

Andrew apparently needed no further confirmation. This was a crisis in his own life which catapulted him for the rest of his long life into the deep walk in the Spirit for which he had yearned and prayed. At this time his father visited him at Worcester and thanked God that he was allowed to be present and speak at such meetings. He said, "Andrew, my son, I have longed for such times as these, which the Lord has let you have."

The same eyewitness tells of a lady who was visiting his parents at the time of these meetings, who later married one of the first missionaries from the area and after long, faithful service died on the mission field:

> Miss Hessie Bosman was cautioned not to go to the meetings because she was in rather weak health. She replied, "No, I must go, even if it should prove my death; for I have prayed so much for these meetings and longed so much to take part, that I cannot remain away."
> She attended, and was the third to engage in prayer that evening. While she was pouring out her heart, the whole meeting broke forth into prayer, and she fell as if unconscious to the ground. I carried her out to the parsonage, where they were some time in bringing her round. But she had not been taken ill, and was none the worse for attending. The next day, she was herself again.

Not only did the revival sweep mightily over the congregation at Worcester, but the lives of many individuals were permanently transformed.

11

Fruit that Remains

It is by solid spiritual effects and changes in the lives of individuals and in the community that a true work of God can be evaluated. When the revival in South Africa passed the stage of vehement emotion and was running a calmer though deeper course, church leaders attempted to catalog its results, which were, in many cases, little less than revolutionary.

In the town of Montagu, a place noted for its indifference to religion, a tone of seriousness about Christian things permeated the whole community. It was recorded that even those who felt compelled to disapprove of certain features of the revival were obliged to confess that within a few months the general improvement in the conduct of the inhabitants was really wonderful.

In Wellington, which was to be Andrew's later appointment, it was reported to the presbytery that the parish made greater moral and spiritual progress in a few weeks than in the course of its history since its establishment. Other communities echoed that record.

It is well known that all revivals attract superficial persons, that there is some mass influence of one upon another, and there is counterfeit of the real. The church leaders were aware of these dangers and acknowledged that these did not discredit the *genuine* work of the Spirit. They pointed to the great number of persons who were soundly converted at that time—some, open sinners; some, respectable churchgoers who, in the sudden light of God's Spirit, realized their own hypocrisy and depravity and repented with overwhelming reality and permanence.

The story was documented of a certain farmer well-known for his quiet and retiring disposition, who hardly ever joined in common conversation because of his shyness. Joyously converted during the revival, he was later visited by some of his former friends who had not known of his conversion. They were amazed when this silent man began to witness to them in a bold and deeply earnest and eloquent manner and "with searching look" about the old truths which, through the enlightenment of the Holy Spirit, suddenly became new to him.

The revival affected all ranks without distinction of age or color. Many youths were touched. Those who had been motivated solely by pleasure and were indifferent to the church, after conversion immediately became involved in Christian ministries. The young people were especially burdened for their still unconverted relatives and friends. Whole households came to Christ through the witness of youths and children.

Nor was the revival limited to the Europeans. Native Africans living on lonely farms as day laborers, often looked down upon by the rest of the population, were equally touched by the Holy Spirit. A certain native girl in the employment of a farmer's wife was overheard in the fields by the farmer as she wept and implored God to forgive her sins in the name of Jesus Christ. On returning home, he inquired if she had previously shown any interest in her soul. His wife replied, "The girl asked me just yesterday if Christ died for her as well as white people, and whether she, too, might ask for pardon and peace with God."

Emma wrote to her mother about the meetings: "We are having so many visitors from surrounding places who come to see us on account of the revival. They go away blessed saying that the half had never been told. It is a solemn thing to live in such a congregation at such a time. I feel sure the Lord is going to bless us even more and yet some things are painful. . . . In the early stage, Andrew came down the aisle and prayed a most solemn, heart-searching prayer that if the work was not of God, He Himself would put a stop to it. The people were terrified as the excitement was very intense. Some even fainted. . . . Andrew is so very discreet in dealing with souls; about twenty came forward last night and others stayed behind to be talked to. We do feel and realize the power and presence of God so mightily. His Spirit is indeed poured out upon us. My little ones are very good so I am able to get out almost every night to the meetings. Andrew is very tired after the meetings but is generally able to sleep well and feels refreshed in the morning."

Not only were the more privileged congregations of the West touched by the Spirit, but the fire spread during 1861 throughout the Central Karroo and beyond, even reviving congregations without pastors. It was indeed not a work of man. Although no single man instigated the revival, Andrew Murray contributed in a large degree to the diffusion of the blessings of the revival. The Lord assured him that he was in the midst of a genuine work of the Spirit, and he allowed himself to be transformed in a deep, inward way.

He began to express that power in his ministry that was obviously different from the intense zeal with which he had already so faithfully served the Lord. He had not been taught to let the Lord work through him, rather than do the tasks of God in his own human power. A man who heard Andrew preach for the first time wrote, "Much has been told us of the talents of that young preacher, but our tense expectation was far surpassed. We cannot but reiterate the heartfelt conviction that it would be the greatest of blessings for the Dutch Reformed Church of South Africa if she possessed a dozen Andrew Murrays of Graaff-Reinet to give to the church as many and suchlike sons as he has given."

At the time Andrew took the Worcester pastorate only one or two of the oldest members were bold enough to pray aloud in meetings, nor was it permissible for women to speak up in prayer meetings. Youth were not affected in their inner lives or lifestyles by the established church. No one would be so presumptive as to declare he was sure he was converted or regenerated. But with the coming of the revival, it was said, "there was a general movement among the dead bones."

Andrew's preaching took on an intangible supernatural quality that was in very deed "in the ministration of the Spirit and of power." It was as though one of the prophets of old had risen from the dead.

Andrew wrote after the revival: "Oh, if we did not so often hinder Him with our much serving, and *much trying to serve*, how surely and mightily would He accomplish *His own work* of renewing souls into the likeness of Christ Jesus. What secrets He would whisper in the silence of a waiting heart. . . . To my mind, the most striking proof that we truly had the Holy Spirit among us in the late movement is to be seen in what He is *now* doing in stirring up in the hearts of believers a desire after more entire *surrender* to Himself and His service." His book *Absolute Surrender* was seeded in what he observed in this arena of experience.

So many young converts came out of the revival that Andrew was burdened with the need to instruct them how not to lose the blessed intimate relationship with Jesus Christ when they inevitably stepped back into their routine lives and duties. He wrote *Abide in Christ* to meet that need, and at once it became a much-beloved companion for many heaven-bound pilgrims.

Around this period he also published a book for those whose weak faith needed strengthening, titled in English *Why Do You Not Believe?*

12

Urban Parish and Court Battles

The synod of the Dutch Reformed Church of South Africa in 1862 honored Andrew by electing him as moderator, though he was only thirty-four years old. This was a distinguished mark of confidence in him by the ministers and elders because the difficulties of the synod that year and in the few years following, in the struggle with the civil courts, were monumental and the decisions made history.

During this period assaults were made upon both the doctrine and the constitution of the church. The rationalistic or "liberal" movement had arisen, which was all-powerful in Holland. It exercised a subtle but profound influence over the minds of the young South African ministers who received their theological training in the universities of Holland. "Liberal" propaganda was everywhere, not only in church journals but even in public newspapers. The constitution and government of the church was open to attack because of its position as an established church which derived its powers and legal authority from its connection with the state.

These were difficult years for Andrew officially and personally, causing tension and consuming the energies of a great many of the leaders involved, especially when it went so far as to necessitate lawsuits in court. One was even against Andrew personally. In the course of three years, however, it seemed that the "liberal" movement had spent its force in the South African Dutch Reformed Church, but not without causing much havoc among the congregations which in many cases were wounded and split.

That this happened right after the sweeping work of a revival with its spiritually unifying love should be no surprise. Satan is always on hand with vicious attempts to nullify the work of God. But the Enemy was not successful. God's work in the hearts of men continued to flow through His surrendered channels, including Andrew.

In 1864 Andrew was called to fill the vacancy in a joint pastorate in Cape Town. He commented, "If God wills to bless, no instrument is too weak, and blessed it is to be the instrument which He condescends to use." His two fellow pastors were men of advancing age, and Andrew found himself plunged into a round of many duties which made heavy and ceaseless demands upon his strength.

During his pastorate at Cape Town, in 1866, Andrew was delegated to go to England in charge of his denomination's appeal to the British Privy Council, as part of his duties as moderator of the synod. Emma and the children, now five, sailed with him. Shortly after their arrival they received the news of the death of Andrew's father who had retired a few months previously because of age and growing weakness. He had served the church faithfully for forty-four years. The Murrays were away ten months, during which time a sixth child, a second son, Andrew Haldane, was born.

To show a humorous side to his sternness, an anecdote is told about Andrew preaching in England to two hundred thieves, probably in a prison, on Christmas day. A captive audience, literally, who had not invited him, they began to cough him down when he began to preach. Taking out his watch, he said, "One at a time, gentlemen, one at a time. As the sailor said to the minister while his donkey brayed, 'Either you or the donkey!' So I will give *you* five minutes to cough and you will give *me* five minutes to preach."

At the end of Andrew's five minutes the men were so interested they forgot to cough any more until the service was ended.

Emma felt very much at home in England since she had many relatives there to visit. During the European trip, Andrew was invited to preach in many prestigious pulpits and halls of learning. That a man of Andrew's judgment knew what he was doing when he refused the call to stay in London is evident. When Emma asked whether he would accept any of the calls, he replied, "No, my church needs me, my people need me, South Africa needs me. I must sacrifice myself for them." He never spoke of it again as a sacrifice, but threw himself heartily into every sphere of work the Lord opened before him.

The congregation in Cape Town was an immense one, consisting of more than 3,000 communicant members and some 5,000 adherents. There were two church buildings, one able to seat 3,000 and the other about 1,000. Three ministers preached in the two churches in rotation. It was said of Andrew that "he speedily realized much more could be done" and he turned immediately to the less privileged classes who lived in more remote districts of the city. There were already schools and weekly chapel services, but Andrew wanted to make the activities more productive spiritually.

He was gifted in inspiring others and putting them to work. He wrote an article in the newspaper on the principles of slum work, which he had learned in Edinburgh. He made the analogy that churches are not like bars, where it is enough to throw open the doors and the longing for drink draws people in. The poor and lost, on the other hand, must be searched for and brought into church. He pointed out that this was not a job for the minister but a labor for Christian laymen, each in charge of certain districts for visitation. "Merely to build schools and churches for the poor is to offer them stones for bread. There must be *living, loving* Christian workers who, like Elisha of old, must take the dead into their arms and prayerfully clasp them close until they come to life again."

He was additionally burdened for the spiritual and intellectual welfare of young men, and in August 1865 became the first president of the Young Men's Christian Association. He was elected over and over and served the Y.M.C.A. productively for many years. Andrew's public, community, and ecclesiastical image grew but not without some envy and opposition. A satirical piece appeared in print about him, which was probably quite an accurate appraisal of his abilities.

One of the men of the ultra-orthodox party, who pose as watchmen on the walls of Zion, is Rev. A. Murray—a worthy leader. Eloquent, quick, and talented, he has an acute mind and clear judgment. He instantly knows the weak points of his opponents' arguments and knows how to assail them. He carries the meeting with him; he is too clever for most. He understands the art of making his ideas so attractive to the elders and the small minds among the ministers (who all look up to him with reverence) that they very seldom venture to contradict Demosthenes, or as another has called him, Apollos. It would be sacrilege to raise a voice against the Right Reverend, the Actuarius, Andrew Murray. There is no member of the Assembly who possesses more influence than he, and certainly no one among the conservatives who better deserves his influence. He is consistent, and consistency always demands respect.

As to his pulpit manner, Andrew was a powerful presence, and his congregation observed that "bookboard and Bible were soundly belabored." But his personal teaching manner with his catechumens was intensely personal. One of his pupils, later a minister, Rev. C. Rabie, tells us how it was:

"I was one of those privileged to be confirmed by Mr. Murray. He always turned us to the Bible and made us read and explain all the answers. Every time the class was over, he asked two or three to remain and he had a personal talk with them about the condition of their souls. Many of us date our spiritual birth from those talks."

Apparently his pastoral visitation was not tea-and-cakes and chatting-about-the-weather, but "carried terror to the hearts of his parishioners," Mr. Rabie went on.

"If his preaching was like thunderbolts from the summit of Sinai, what would personal rebuke be like? Under his individual dealings with them, people felt that they were being ground to powder—in a loving way. On one occasion, at the close of a prayer meeting, Mr. Murray proceeded to deal with each individual present. One lady, observing how her pastor drew nearer and nearer to where she sat, became gradually more and more uneasy, until, as Mr. Murray turned to her, she fell upon her knees crying, 'O Lord, into Thy hands I commend my spirit!'"

Mr. Rabie added that there was a great contrast between the stern young Mr. Murray of those days and the loving and gentle Mr. Murray whom they knew in later years. God was dealing with His servant differently during each period of his life, and Andrew in turn dealt differently with his people as his own experiences matured and mellowed him.

About this stern period, one of his daughters sought to give us a more balanced view of his temperament. She recalled winter evenings when her father would read to the children and dramatize for the younger ones the roars of the lions in missionary adventure stories, "which would cause us great but laughing terror." He took wild romps with his youngsters in the open fields, and on summer afternoons the parents would take the children for a picnic in the hills to engage in games such as throwing stones at a bottle. They recalled the excitement and joy of very human and emotional reunions when their father returned from long journeys.

During his Cape Town pastorate, Andrew began to devote himself more continuously to literary work. *Be Merciful Unto Me*, a series of devotional studies appearing first in magazine form and then in a book for seekers, was a study in the Fifty-first Psalm. A series of papers followed, titled *God's Word and Error*, but was not finished into a book. He also edited a Christian magazine for several years, one in which some of his own writings were published.

The church work in Cape Town did not prosper up to Andrew's expectations due to the system of three pastors, and in 1871 he received a call to a pastorate at Wellington, forty-five miles distant. While he was considering whether to go, his brother John wrote him, bringing out several considerations that might influence him to stay in Cape Town.

Andrew wrote him back, "That just goes to show how each of us must, in the final, decide for himself. The very things which you think would influence me to stay, do not weigh with me at all. I don't mind the difficult situation of the Wellington congregation; nor to have all kinds of people, old and young, under my continuous personal influence. Systematic preaching and care of one congregation are to my liking. Neither charge throws much into the scale of a possibly better place for a more prolonged life. To possess fixed property here somehow doesn't appear to weigh with me. If it be God's will that I go, He will provide in this matter.

"The argument of someone else that I am indispensable here as representing the church does not appear to reach me. My first work, my calling, is to be a pastor. Where I can be happy in this work, thither I feel myself drawn. But I do think that I have honestly and in childlike simplicity said to the Father that if He would have me stay here, I am ready and willing."

It was thus that Andrew waited upon the Lord for every decision. He was quietly confident: "I dare not think that God will leave me to my own devices."

13

Pastorate in a Pasture

Andrew did accept the Wellington pastorate in 1871. Many people in the Cape Town church felt sure that Andrew would not leave because at age forty-three he was "on his way up" and would soon become Sr. minister with ever greater prestige and influence. Some looked upon his decision as a backward step on the road to fame. Why should he choose the small congregation at Wellington with its limitations and leave the glitter of the city and its opportunities for advancement?

But God's ways are not our ways, nor His thoughts our thoughts. It was that very quiet, contemplative, country life in Wellington that led to a deeper, truer knowledge of God and ultimately to the writing of the many Christian books by which he has become a blessing to God's people in all lands. God chose for His servant a less active and less prominent public role. By "pruning" him and cutting back his labors, God enabled Andrew to bear much fruit. Surely Andrew reflected on these ways of God as he wrote the book *The True Vine*, with its deep spiritual implications.

"Why call Mr. Murray to our church?" an old farmer of the Wellington congregation remarked. "In two years we will have the expenses of another funeral." Strenuous labor in past charges and the strife of the synod with the civil courts had left their physical marks on Andrew, so he may have looked too frail to last long. But his spirit was robust and exercised, ever deepening his own soul's journey and broadening his influence among men.

The satisfaction of preaching to his own congregation year after year also proved more beneficial in spite of the hard work to which he committed himself. Andrew was in his prime, and in God's providence was to spend his remaining forty-five years of life at Wellington, thirty-four of them as pastor.

In contrast to the urban setting of Cape Town, Wellington was described by a visitor as "beauty in the lap of grandeur." A panorama of mountain ranges with rugged peaks, bathed in the setting sun with exquisite rose and purple tints, awed even those who dwelt there from childhood. The lush valleys were lined with vineyards; orchards climbed the hill slopes with their lavish foliage, blossoms, and fruit. The ground was exceptionally fertile and the farms were comparatively small but yielding abundantly.

The village itself sheltered only about 4,000 inhabitants, white and colored, but it was the center of a larger, prosperous farming community. Andrew's congregation was also a contrast from his previous charges. Composed largely of descendants of the Huguenots who fled from persecution in France, they were, in some sense, refugees. French names were as common as Dutch. A deeply religious people, they faithfully attended the services. Especially since the recent revival, many were zealous for spiritual matters.

Wherever the Murrays served, their parsonage became a center of hospitality. Wellington was no exception. Ever since the mountain pass between Worcester and Wellington was opened, communication was easy and the distance not formidable. It also lay on the main road connecting Cape Town with all northern settlements. With a roomy parsonage, streams of visitors were common.

Andrew was immediately plunged into many congregational problems and activities—the liquidation of the church debt, higher education, the training of teachers, local mission work, and church government matters. But he loved his people, making no distinction between the poorest and most ignorant and the rich and wise.

Generally they were simple folk, not highly trained academically but full of practical knowledge of their work and good sense. As Jesus had done, Andrew drew upon the daily lives of his people to illustrate spiritual truths in his preaching, teaching, and most surely in his writing.

His book *The True Vine* was first preached then written with the foremost occupation of his people in mind. We can visualize Andrew visiting his parishioners and being shown their vineyards. He asked questions on the nature of vine growth and the husbandman's duties. Afterward he prayed and meditated to receive lessons from God.

But it was this very occupation that some thought would cause an open controversy. His congregation was not acquainted with the temperance principles which Andrew held staunchly throughout his ministry. Soon after he arrived, he started a crusade to close down some of the many public taverns.

"Mr. Murray, you are going to split the congregation!" warned an angry wine farmer.

"Never," Andrew replied. "We will, if necessary, take the scissors of love and cut it in two, having one side for temperance and the other not, but we *will* live together in *love*." He approached them tactfully, again using illustrations with which they were familiar.

"When a farmer trains a young horse, it will often shy at a stone or something else. The wise farmer will quietly lead the horse to the unfamiliar object and let him look at it and smell it till all fear passes and it will not shy anymore. So I will not force temperance upon you. But we will speak and preach about it until you are familiar with it and approve of it!"

He was successful—the number of saloons dwindled to only four in Wellington, whereas there were, at the same period, forty in the next village.

But his crusade was not without militant opposition. Many people were angry with him and someone tried to burn the parsonage down by throwing lighted kerosene-soaked rags into their windows near the lace curtains. God overshadowed them with His protection.

Andrew was genuinely interested and involved in the advancement of all community causes, whether they were related to religion or not. Through the years, many of his opponents became his warm friends. Even when men opposed him, he still maintained sympathy and communication with them.

In his new location he initiated some of the similar, successful projects he established in Cape Town, among them the training of the members of his congregation to do mission work in the different wards of his parish. He continued to be burdened for the large number of colored people—day laborers, farm servants, household workers, herdsmen and the like—who were still unreached for Christ by ongoing gospel work. To provide for the spiritual benefit of this neglected group, Andrew started Sunday Schools and evening schools for the old and young with good attendance both in the church mission hall and in the out-districts of the congregation, until they spread to nearly every ward. His conviction was that their own farm people could never be reached properly for Christ unless the masters were also helpers to instruct the servants about the gospel. The colored people showed great eagerness for these opportunities.

Although concentrating on one congregation, Andrew was in continual demand as an evangelist and accepted invitations to conduct other meetings as he was able. He trained his own congregation as a "backup team" to help in his work by prayer. Many of his writings, such as *The Ministry of Intercession* and *The Prayer Life* had their foundation in these instructions. He wrote back to his people from a meeting, "I feel anxious to get God's people together to point out the need of intercession and entire consecration. . . . I have a strong feeling that God will give our people the spirit of prayer to ask and expect new and more mighty blessings when I return. . . . I beseech you to pray for a more powerful work of the Holy Spirit. . . . Stir up the people to pray for us."

Andrew was quick to enlist prayer partners for God's Kingdom, believing prayer to be the only channel to secure the workings of God in the lives of men. When a number of retired farmers came to live in the village, Andrew suggested that God brought them there to become intercessors and set about to train them for that work. He was an example to the believers by his own consecration.

His famous prayer for himself was:

"May not a single moment of my life be spent outside the light, love, and joy of God's presence. And not a moment without the entire surrender of myself as a vessel for Him to fill full of His Spirit and His love."

Andrew tried never to preach what he did not practice, especially in the area of prayer. Andrew's habit was to write in a small book the subjects for which he was making special prayer requests. Opposite each were recorded the answers from God. A recurring request was "for the power of the Spirit in all my work, *that it not be done in my own strength.*"

Another was "That I may endeavor in preaching to make clear this truth of main importance: that conversion is surrender of sin—of *all* sin."

And in the middle of a building program of the seminary: "Let me feel that when once I have cast my cares upon Thee, they are Thy concerns and not mine, and that Thou wilt do all for me. May I have grace with stones and bricks and wood, with all the burdens and workmen, to trust and pray and rest in Thy faithfulness who never fails."

An intimate prayer was jotted down on a back page: "Infinite God, make me empty and then fill me full of Thy Holy Spirit and love, full to overflowing, that this weary world may see and drink. Full of Thy love to me, full of love to Thee, full of love to them, to everyone."

The golden ray of prayer illumined all Andrew did. Like Luther, he believed that nothing that was amiss and demanded correction could not be corrected or endured by prayer. The striving of his human spirit to attain, particularly through prayer, to the blessedness of daily and uninterrupted communion with God may be seen as the secret of Andrew's spiritual strength.

Andrew was aware that concerning prayer there are two sides to the question: Does *prayer change things* (the objective influence of God) or is the main value of prayer that it *changes the people that pray* (the reflex influence upon us)? Andrew took the position that although the exercise of prayer can either calm us into peace or raise us into ecstasy in the presence of the Father, yet this is *not* the teaching of our Savior. "If we carefully study all that our Lord spoke of prayer, we shall see that everywhere He urges and encourages us to *offer definite petitions* and *expect definite answers.*"

In 1883 Andrew founded the *Bible and Prayer Union*, the main object being to encourage members of his church to read the Scriptures daily and pray regularly for specific causes. Each member received for a mere shilling a year an annual calendar with daily lessons and a prayer list as well as some useful book. The Union started on a modest scale, but its membership increased to 20,000. Expenses were met, and it brought spiritual support and blessing to thousands throughout the country. For more than forty years Andrew was the editor of its daily devotional, *Uit de Beek* (Out of the Spring).

There was a very deep work of grace in many hearts at Wellington so that a large proportion of the congregation was truly seeking to live for God. Many of their most sacred experiences centered around the remarkable communion services held in the church. One of Murray's daughters later described them.

"Can one ever forget the times when 500 or 600 communicants would gather around the Lord's Table, and the holy influence of the Lord that permeated the church! Can we forget the holy awe, the deep reverence, the joy and often the rapture written on father's face when 'Heaven came down our souls to meet'?

"I remember once that father seemed to have really been taken up to the third heaven and such a deep solemnity rested on us all before he spoke again with the words, 'I live, yet not I, but Christ liveth in me, and that life which I now live in the flesh, I live in *faith*, the *faith* which is in the Son of God *who loved me* and gave himself for me.' More especially father emphasized those words '*who loved me.*' Oh the wonder of it that we so little understand! Let us love Him and trust Him more and more!

"We left the Table feeling that we had indeed been fed on heavenly manna, and rose with a deeper love and fuller determination to do and dare all for our adorable Lord and Master. We were strengthened and refreshed as with new wine, and in the Thanksgiving Service afterward there was a time of wondrous praise, not from the lips alone, but from the heart."

Andrew's holy and important estimation of the sacrament of The Lord's Table is set forth in a deeply beautiful and biblical way in his book by that title. He communicated the same value of it to his people and was most grieved when congregations took lightly their participation in that service.

During this early period at Wellington, the Murray family both decreased and increased, by joys and sorrows. Because there were few suitable high schools for girls in South Africa, the Murrays decided to send their two eldest daughters, Emmie and Mary, ages 14 and 13, to the Moravian Institution at Zeist in Holland for two years. Their father carried on a detailed correspondence to encourage and instruct them, doubtless remembering his own need for such when his brother John and he left the family circle as youngsters to study in Scotland. He wrote to them tenderly on their level, recounting things they would be interested in and instructing them about common matters. A few excerpts will show his love and care:

> Dearest child, we have been asking the Lord this morning, should you perhaps feel somewhat sad and desolate on your birthday today, that you will be led to feel that Jesus is near. Do try to get and keep hold of the precious truth that there is *no friend like Jesus* and that even when we feel naughty and foolish or sinful, He still loves us and wants us to come to Him with all our troubles, that He may heal and comfort us. . . .
>
> I hope that the difficulties that trouble you will gradually smooth down. But remember, when difficulties won't accommodate themselves to your wishes, there is nothing like you accommodating yourself to them! This is part of true wisdom and in time takes away the unpleasantness. . . . Don't forget, the object of school life is not so much to impart a large amount of information, but to cultivate those powers by which you can, afterwards, gain information for yourself. And for the calling out of these powers and the cultivation of the habit of application and careful thinking, those studies are useful in which the feeling of interest and pleasure appears to be sacrificed to a sense of duty.
>
> When traveling up a hill last week, one of my companions was criticizing a road, and pointing out how much better it might have

been made. When we got a little farther up the hill, we saw that he was wrong. People at the foot of a hill cannot understand the reason for all the windings of the road, but as they rise higher they discover them. You are just now only beginning to climb: follow in trust the path by which you are led. Afterwards you will understand better than you do now. . . .

You seem to have some difficulties to see true children of God, your classmates, indulging in conversation or other activities which appear to you wrong. Ask Jesus to help *you* to act up to the light of *your* conscience. If their conscience is not fully enlightened on a point, that may be an excuse for *them*, but cannot be for *you*.

Try and think, my dear little girls, that you are not too small to exercise influence. Your Uncle John and I thought so too when young, but we found we did exercise some considerable influence in matters among our young friends. Don't argue with others and don't condemn them, but simply try to show that there is a way of being engaged in religious exercises all day without being sad or unhappy, and invite them to join you in such things as reading and singing.

I ordered for you immediately some good books for your Sabbath reading, and to loan to your friends. . . .

The weather is beautiful now that spring has come, and Papa has begun his gardening. It has been perfectly exquisite to be out-of-doors. I think how pleased I shall be when my girls come back and I can show them what a nice garden I have succeeded in making.

Love the Lord Jesus very much, and do love each other fervently and be very gentle toward each other as the Bible says."

Sorrow did not pass the Murrays by. One of the Murray daughters, only eight months old, died just before their departure for England in 1866. While their two daughters were abroad, two more little ones, Fanny and Willie, died from illness the same year. Andrew had to console his absent children in Holland, as well as himself, his wife and the other children.

In beautiful trust and acceptance of God's perfect plan, they all confirmed their own surrender to the Lord again.

In November of the following year, a new son was born to the Murrays, and Andrew shared the joyous news by correspondence with his absent daughters.

Whenever Andrew passed through some special experience, joyful, difficult, sad or perplexing, he was always attentive to what the Lord was teaching him. He felt that it was generally a call to some special writing, or to some new service for the Lord. The death of his little daughters and son became to him a fresh call to teach his people to evangelize and train their children and the children and youth of his country. It turned out that a great work of Christian education was launched by Andrew's new vision.

14

Commit to Faithful Persons

The most important ministry Andrew undertook in the early days of his Wellington pastorate had to do with the chronic question of supplying the need for more laborers for the Lord's harvest. He received the insight from God that the normal, logical, and most available ongoing source was *from the Christian homes of his own country* rather than continually depending on resources of personnel from abroad.

Although avidly recruiting what we may term "full-time Christian workers," Andrew had a definite philosophy about every believer's responsibility before God. "Every Christian is called to be a worker for God. The secret of a truly religious education is to train our sons with *this* as the great thought of their lives—that they not only belong to the Lord, but each one must work for Him. Work for Him must be the *main object*, not a *side issue*. In whatever position or business they are, they must know that they live only to serve the Lord, and to say of *all* their money, their influence, their talents, 'I hold my life every hour at Thy command!'"

In the denominational magazine he wrote a series of articles which were widely circulated and influential. He made an irresistible appeal to all Christian parents in the land to consecrate their children to God's service and be willing to let the Lord call them to the home and foreign field for Christian service as well as to other occupations.

He answered every objection that the parents might have. He pointed out that the Lord has a right to our children, the Lord needs our children, and will Himself indicate to the believers which children He would have and could use. He answered the excuse of parents that they had no money to educate their children; and the excuse that their children may not have the necessary abilities; and the excuse of having an only child or that some had only daughters.

On this latter point, God gave Andrew new insights which were ahead of his times and greatly forward-looking in what might perhaps be considered a backward land. "Is there no place in the special service of God for our daughters?" He maintained that there most certainly was, but even if there wasn't, he declared, "The consecration of your daughters to God can never be a vain and idle matter. The Lord has lately shown that He can use women to perform great and important services for His Church, and if parents will present their daughters to the Lord, He will know how to prepare a sphere of work for them. It may be as intercessors for others, as laborers in His Kingdom, in nursing the sick, or in caring for the poor. Parents who train their daughters with this in view, in faith and prayer, will surely experience that their labor is not vain in the Lord."

Andrew singled out a special capacity in which women can work for the Lord: teaching and general education by Christians of firm conviction. There were many teachers, he pointed out, who just teach to earn their living and don't really care for the spiritual lives of the children. "May the day soon dawn when many of the young women of our church, with training, will devote themselves to feeding the lambs solely at the impulse of the love of Jesus." This was a banner plea for Christian education which Andrew did not feel should be left in the wishful-thinking stage.

"What are you reading that engrosses you so, Andrew?" asked Emma one day during Christmas vacation. "I can hardly rouse you for mealtime."

"Oh Emma, the example of this book urges me to a mountain task. I can hardly wait to start climbing!"

Knowing how to spark Emma's curiosity, he added, "Moreover, it is about a woman."

Emma picked up the book from Andrew's lap and read, *The Life History and Work of Mary Lyon*. "And who is she?"

"The founder of the Ladies' Seminary at Mount Holyoke in Massachusetts in the United States. (It is known today as Mt. Holyoke College.) One day we must go to America and see that institution for ourselves. It is just the kind of thing that South Africa needs. By God's enabling, *we shall have it!*"

With Emma's eager and faithful writing help, another series of articles was born from Andrew's heart, published in the church magazine at intervals during 1873.

Andrew could not wait for the dragging feet of others to initiate such an important task. He was already at work on a practical plan to establish at Wellington a similar institution which would be openly Christian with an entirely Christian faculty and domestic duties performed by the pupils themselves. The fees would be small enough that even the lower income families could afford to send their children.

On June 25, 1873, the Huguenot Seminary to train young girls for educational work was founded. The members of his congregation responded heartily to their pastor's project. Funds were raised from many places including Andrew's travels for that purpose. The formal opening took place in January 1874.

Young ladies began to arrive from all parts of the country both to teach and to learn. When classes started, the building was already too small and a wing was added immediately. Exploding enrollment necessitated still another new building. Two thousand people attended the opening ceremony, and congratulatory letters and telegrams poured in from a distance. So successful was the undertaking that it attracted widespread attention. Even visitors from other countries came to see it.

Several teachers from America, Holland, and England gave the faculty a good academic standing, and the standards of the curriculum were high, comparing favorably to the best institutions for training teachers. Andrew had adopted Mary Lyon's maxim with zest, and it took hold everywhere: "First the Kingdom of God; after that, most certainly, all science and knowledge."

Andrew had been bold to ask for a teacher directly from Mount Holyoke to be sent to South Africa, guaranteeing her salary; they sent two, who were the excellent pioneers of the whole project. To crown the success of the first year, many of the girls who were not Christians when they enrolled had definitely been won to Christ.

In visiting down-country congregations, Andrew was shocked to see "how much ground we have already lost with young people by the influence of worldly teachers, and we have not an hour to lose if we want by means of pious teachers to win the younger generations for the Lord. Oh, what a tragedy that Christ's lambs are given to the charge of the world!"

Andrew engaged in many "collecting tours" during the early years of the Huguenot Seminary. Andrew's philosophy on money raising may be summed up in his words: "My brothers, if this is God's work, He surely has enough money to dispense. When He has opened heart and mouth and eye, He will not leave the hands closed. When a matter is made plain to our congregations, they give willingly. . . . It is God's part to care for the money, and ours to discover what the will of the Lord is and what work we ought to perform for Him—and then in faith to begin it."

But Andrew's travels were multipurpose, which he sums up in a letter home: "The collections were fair, the interest in consecrating children to the service of the Lord fair, the meetings not without fruit, the preaching not unblessed." But Andrew's call from God was far from giving fund-raising a high priority. He was a pastor and an evangelist first. This caused a struggle in his own heart.

He wrote his wife: "The more I travel, the more I see that the *great* need of our church is *evangelists*. And though I cannot in the least see it would be possible for me to give up Wellington or to arrange for long absences, it does almost appear wrong not to undertake the work of evangelism when one knows there are hundreds ready to be brought in. It appears terrible to let them go on in darkness and indecision when they are willing to be helped.

"I have been much struck in reading the notes on Exodus by the words of God to Pharaoh: 'Let my people go that they may serve me.' God does hear the cry and sighing of the thousands of seeking ones and wants His servants to lead them out of bondage. And how can I help saying that if He will use me, I shall only consider the honor too high. It makes me sad to preach one or two earnest evangelistic sermons, to see the impression made, and to go away feeling sure that if I could devote a little more time and individual attention to the work, many souls would come to light and joy."

That gave Andrew increasing discomfort about spending even as much time as he did on fund-raising. "The thought suggests itself whether, with such precious opportunities so short and rare, it is right to preach a sermon in order to get a collection, no matter how worthy the project. May the Lord direct and guide. We have said and do say that *entire* consecration to His work and will is our choice and our life. And we know that for all difficulties and questions that come, we have an infallible solution in the assurance that Christ who lives our life in us is sufficient for all that comes and will guide and keep us in perfect peace."

There were times when he apparently did not meet the high quota of funds which he expected, and some questioned whether that particular journey had been the Lord's will. Andrew gave us an excellent insight into his views on success and failure when looking at anything from God's vantage point.

"You think because I have not been so successful that this is a sign that the journey is not the Lord's will? I think we must be careful in judging thus. Either failures or successes are sometimes our most dangerous temptations sent to test our principle. We cannot judge our path by this, for God may have sent it to try us.

"The great thing is to have our minds always in a childlike state when we are considering or fixing our plans; thus we shall know that God is guiding our path, even if it were a mistaken one, to very blessed issues. Failure—though perhaps I ought not to call it failure, even though I have not got quite as much collection as last time—even comparative failure has not for one moment made me think I was not in the right path.

"But one thing has been very heavy on me all through—the idea of being on a mission for *money* and having no time or opportunity to work for souls."

Finally he rested in his own recommitment: "I have this day sought to lay myself afresh on the altar and to look to the Great High Priest presenting me to the Father, an acceptable and accepted sacrifice, and engaging by His Holy Spirit to appropriate and use the sacrifice. The need and want of dealing with souls rests heavy upon me. But whether there is any prospect of *my* doing the work, I cannot say. Or whether by training *others*—workers, teachers and missionaries—the Lord may permit me to do *more*, I don't know. But it is just so sad to see souls by multitudes seeking and not finding, sighing and not helped, apparently because there is none to show them the way of the Lord!"

Andrew ultimately realized that by providing the Christian training opportunities for those who would be pastors, teachers and evangelists in the future, he was *reproducing himself and his own vision and zeal*, and accomplishing more for God's Kingdom than if he decided to drop everything and do evangelistic work alone.

God gave His servant Andrew enough days to accomplish each of the different callings on his life and ministry which God ordained. His longing to devote himself fully as an evangelist was certainly satisfied and crowned with tremendous spiritual success at an age when most men feel their life work is finished. In his most advanced years he was led to break through the conventions of a lifetime and get into personal touch with seeking souls of any age group. He continually gathered whitened harvests for his Lord. Because Andrew was able to spiritually discern God's will and personal priorities for his ministry at each point in his life, he did not haphazardly abandon any clear call from the Lord to jump into another, no matter with what intense urgency it was laid before him. "Waiting upon God" was truly the hallmark of his life, expressed richly in his book by that title.

Andrew was influenced at this time by the revivals and evangelistic movements in other lands. He asked the Lord how the lessons learned from these movements and men of God might be adapted to the South African situation. He received from Edinburgh an account of the work of D. L. Moody in America with reports of his addresses and statement of his methods. He prayed over and discussed these things with other pastors and co-workers, particularly the possibility of beginning "after-meetings" of a type which D. L. Moody employed.

Again, waiting on God was his watchword. He held back in launching these until God had given them all clear assurance that this should be done. It was not until after ten days of prayer meetings with his own church, pleading with the Lord for a moving among the unsaved, that he began to hold such after-meetings. The Lord blessed immeasurably in the next five weeks of evangelistic services where workers were in the church until late at night dealing with anxious inquirers.

15

"Quite a Lion" in America

Andrew's first trip to America was in 1877 in connection with his reelection as moderator of the synod and his representation of the Dutch Reformed Church at the Pan-Presbyterian Council meeting in Edinburgh, Scotland. His younger brother Charles, who had succeeded their father as minister of the church in Graaff-Reinet, accompanied him and the other appointee, Rev. Colin Fraser. For Charles it was a breathtaking first trip to both continents, and he kept a journal of their whirlwind schedule. He was much impressed by the important people in Christian and educational fields whom they were meeting everywhere, and the famous pulpits and meetings to which his brother was invited.

"On Andrew's back," he wrote home, "not literally but metaphorically, *I* get in anywhere! In the circles in which we move, Andrew is quite a lion!"

After the council was finished, Andrew had several additional goals for his tour—to see the condition of the Church and education, and the state of the spiritual life in each country. He looked forward with the greatest pleasure to meet some of the men whom God raised up as "witnesses of what He can do for His children." He hoped to see the work of Moody and Sankey since "grey-haired ministers in England

and Scotland have acknowledged how much they have learned from these men. And there are other evangelists who have not exactly received a ministerial training but whose enthusiasm and gifts have in many instances been highly instructive to those who are engaged in the regular ministry of the Word."

He wanted to observe what was being done in another area for which he had been burdened in his personal ministry. "What endeavors are there to lead those who are already within the fold to *a deeper comprehension of Christian truth and privilege?* If there is one thing which the Church needs, it is labor directed to this end. The more we study the state of the Church of Christ on earth, the more is conviction strengthened that it does not answer to its holy calling. Hence the powerlessness of the Church against unbelief and semi-belief and superstition, against worldliness and sin and heathenism.

"The power of faith, the power of prayer, the power of the Holy Spirit, are all too greatly lacking. God's children, in the first place, require a revival—a new revelation by the Holy Spirit of what is the hope of their calling, of what God does indeed expect from them, and of the life of power and consecration, of joy and fruitfulness, which God has prepared for them in Christ." (His book *The State of the Church* was written during this period.)

Actually, the chief object of his visit to America was to find teachers, above all, lady teachers, for the Huguenot Seminary and its daughter institutions. When he returned to South Africa months later, he brought with him fourteen lady teachers, twelve from America, one from Scotland, one from Holland, as well as the minister brother of one of the pioneer teachers from Mt. Holyoke with his wife and five children. A successful recruiting, indeed!

They saw most of the things which Andrew hoped to see, besides getting acquainted with the Dutch Reformed Church in America and making an eagerly anticipated visit to Mt. Holyoke Seminary. The invitations to speak were so many that Andrew and Charles separated to accept more of them. Charles, understandably in the shadow of Andrew but evidently strong in his affection and respect for his older brother, addressed himself to the students at Amherst College, "You must please understand that I am not *the* Mr. Murray; I am *the other* Mr. Murray!"

As to the just concluded Pan-Presbyterian Council in Scotland, Andrew sent back many reports to the church magazine. He was impressed with the presentation of missions by his esteemed friend Dr. A. Duff of India, to whom he referred as "the prince of modern missionaries."

Andrew reported: "Speaking as one of the prophets of old, Dr. Duff said that he wished to bear witness to one matter especially, namely, that missions are not *one* of the activities of the Church, but the *only* object for which it exists. 'I wish,' said Dr. Duff, 'to take the highest possible Scriptural ground with reference to the sole and supreme duty of the Church of Christ to devote all its strength to this cause. With the exception of the brief apostolic age, there has been no period in the history of the Church when this has been actually done, to the great shame of the Church and the unspeakable loss of this poor world.

"'Holding this conviction, a conviction that has been gathering strength during these past forty years of my life, you will not take it amiss in me, standing as I do upon the verge of the eternal world, when I give expression to my immovable assurance that unless and until this supreme duty is more deeply felt, more powerfully realized, and more implicitly obeyed, not only by individual believers but by the Church at large, we are only playing at missions, deceiving our own selves, slighting the command of our blessed King, and expending in all manner of fruitless struggle the powers, the means, and the abilities which should be devoted with undivided enthusiasm to the spiritual subjugation of the nations.'"

Andrew commented earnestly, "All that I heard, both in America and in Scotland, concerning the missionary enterprise, has wrought in me a deeper conviction that our church has been planted by God in South Africa with the purpose of bringing the gospel to the *native peoples* of the continent of Africa; and that, if this work is to be done, we must have an institution where our sons and daughters can be trained to fulfill it."

With his keen spiritual perception, Andrew made one reference to an unfavorable aspect of the council meetings. "The same observation has frequently been made of our own synodical meetings. When a large number of God's servants meet in order to consult about the interests of His Kingdom and about the work they have to perform in connection with it, one would expect that their first felt need would be to place themselves as servants in the presence of their Lord, and while they wait there in worship and faith, to experience the renewal of those spiritual powers upon which everything depends.

"And yet so frequently it happens that in ecclesiastical and theological gatherings, the so-called ordinary business occupies the first place, while hardly any time can be found for spiritual matters. Though we listened with great pleasure to what was said about the exercise of the spirit of love, about faithfulness to the doctrine of the church, and about the earnestness displayed in the council, more than one of us felt this great lack. I have no doubt that this lack will make itself felt even more in the future."

Andrew's comment is as valid in today's ecclesiastical circles and gatherings as it was more than a hundred years ago, to the spiritual poverty of God's Kingdom. His convictions were written in another of his books, *The Key to the Missionary Problem.*

Andrew attributed to the influence of Moody the fact that even in Scotland and England there was much more readiness now to speak out about one's religion and much more warmth of spirit. "I noticed that the whole religious tone of Scotland has been lifted up and brightened most remarkably. I do praise God for it. Then, too, there is much earnest work being done, though I get the impression in many places that the activity and joy of *work* is regarded too much as the essence of religion. And I see that when I try to speak of the deeper and inner life, many are glad to listen, and confess to a want.

"For myself, I have learned this lesson, that it will not do to press too much on the one side of holiness and communion with Jesus, without the other side of work. There is no joy like that over repentant sinners, no communion closer than 'Go into all the world and teach . . . and lo! I am with you.' Yet the joy of work and of revival is *not* enough. God's children must be led into the secret of the *possibility of unbroken communion* with Jesus personally. I have been much impressed with the need of the union of these two matters, work and communion. . . ." And this point is truly what much of Andrew's writing was about—the balance between abiding and working, the inner life coupled with outward service. Andrew exemplified both in his life. His book *Working for God* was written with those concerns.

After a rather restful voyage home, Andrew jumped right into work connected with his growing church, the Huguenot Seminary, the new Training Institute, the placement of the new teachers, and synodical matters. These combined projects would heavily tax the strength of any man, but at this time of his life Andrew was at the height of his powers of body and brain and spirit. His clear and ready mind and quick grasp of guiding principles enabled him to carry out with ease duties others would scarcely attempt. He was impelled by the assurance that he was about his Father's business and expected his Father to enable him to carry it out.

16

Revival Winds Blow South

Whatever winds were blowing on the European continent and in America, whether intellectual, religious or political, eventually affected the younger, developing countries including South Africa. Most of its influential class received its academic preparation in those countries, and books and magazines flowed from abroad to shape the public mind. Holland, Scotland and England deeply influenced church life and thought.

The Dutch Reformed Church was by far the largest of the denominations in South Africa, with three times as many members as all other Protestant bodies combined. Since it had been freed of its governmental bondage of the early days, many new activities were begun and growth was significant.

Without question, Andrew Murray was the chief and most honored teacher of the Dutch Reformed Church in his generation. In whatever direction he grew in the Lord, whatever truths he grasped from the Word of God and taught, these spread throughout the church. As he formulated his own impressions on what some people called the "higher life," others were drawn upward. However, he did not escape criticism and opposition even from his fellow pastors.

Andrew was continually growing deeper in the Lord, both in his practical experience and teaching concerning the life of sanctification.

He was disappointed that in the Scotland of 1877 so few ministers advanced beyond teaching elementary truths of the Lord. He felt that Christians in general were "terribly afraid of perfectionism." Entire consecration was a point he sought to emphasize. Conferences were springing up, some with Andrew's backing, not only for evangelism but for deepening of the spiritual life of believers, even special conferences for ministers.

One such conference was held at Colesberg in 1879 expressly for the encouragement of ministers in their responsible spiritual tasks. Andrew underscored the value of such meetings in his invitation:

> The blessing consists not merely in the interchange of thought, ... the unity of the Spirit is also experienced more powerfully. [In this larger fellowship] the Spirit of God is found working with power, visions are instantaneously obtained which otherwise would only have come after the lapse of years, and we are strengthened to acts of faith and consecration for which we have longed for many months. . . . Solitude, however indispensable, is not sufficient. God speaks to *companies* of men as He never speaks to *solitary* watchers or students; there is a fuller tone, an intenser fervor, in pentecostal revelations [to a whole body] than in personal communion, and there is a keener job [in group fellowship] than can be realized in the devoutest solitude.

The theme of that conference was "Enduring Joy," and the possibility of living always in such spiritual communion with the Lord as to foster it. However, not all of the ministerial brethren present were convinced that such a life of faith and such undisturbed peace and joy *were* really attainable, feeling it too idealistic. As they studied together, it was brought out that such a life, "although high, was already known to the saints under the old dispensation, and therefore must surely be attainable by saints under the new." The realization of this truth led to more prayer.

Not only were Andrew's teachings on the deeper life not immediately accepted by fellow ministers, but they came under attack in the denominational magazine in a "readers write" debate. His own congregation was closely scrutinized to discover whether his *higher teachings* were exemplified in their *higher conduct*. Critics were quick to jump on any discrepancies, and enemies were poised to attack. Especially was his church watched to see if the members' financial giving was in line with their supposedly generous giving of themselves to the Lord in entire consecration. Andrew's congregation stood up well under this fire.

Great revivals were stirring other countries during this period. D. L. Moody and Ira D. Sankey strongly influenced Great Britain on their remarkable evangelistic trips across the Atlantic. Simple, untheologically educated laymen, they drew immense crowds. Thousands were converted, believers were edified, churches were built up, and most remarkably their unorthodox methods of work were accepted by many who had been most conservative and traditional.

These men never visited South Africa, but the spiritual waves they stirred up broke in force upon her shores. News of their campaigns hit the newspapers and magazines regularly and descriptions of their meetings and results were common conversation everywhere. Persons who returned from Europe or America brought firsthand accounts of the new warmth and glow so many hearts were experiencing. A spirit of high expectancy and prayer arose that God could and would do a similar work among His people anywhere.

And He did! Revivals broke out in Swellendam, Montagu, Wellington, Cape Town, and Stellenbosch. A large number of young people were converted. Special campaigns were arranged by the synod to follow up these young people and conserve the results. Andrew was heavily engaged in such meetings and his church gave him freedom to hold several evangelistic tours within his country.

These "special services," as they were called, were not heard of in the Dutch Reformed Church because meetings were usually conducted only in direct connection with local congregations. Andrew spent considerable time explaining and writing about their purpose to prevent misunderstanding and to gain cooperation.

He assured the people, "No new gospel is being preached . . . but these meetings are to preach solely the message of conversion and faith and to insist on the immediate acceptance of the Lord Jesus as Savior. . . . It is always time to repent and believe, but there are times when the minister seeks to insist with special earnestness upon *today* and *now*. The purpose of special services is nothing else than to shout this *now* in the sinner's ears."

While putting strong emphasis upon the cooperation of churches and Christians in these services—their preparation, visitation, assistance in counseling, and personal witness—Andrew underscored, "*Everything depends upon the Spirit of God* and the measure of faith in which His power is entreated and expected.... Present yourselves to Jesus Christ for His work, that He may gird you about with His Holy Spirit.... Encourage each other to expect great things. Continue steadfastly in secret and united prayer, and see if He will not open to you the windows of heaven and pour you out a blessing so that there shall not be room enough to receive it...."

One of Andrew's trips lasted for two months with meetings held in ten cities. The spiritual results of this series of special services in the wake of the revivals were great and permanent. The work was especially blessed among the children and the youth, not only in the villages and cities but in the different wards of the congregations. The young people often started weekly prayer meetings of their own and were greatly in earnest.

The congregation at Colesberg reported: "... indeed we have cause to shout. 'The Lord hath done great things for us, whereof we are glad.' Believers have been quickened and strengthened and the indifferent aroused and brought to Christ. Youth and age rejoice together in a new-found salvation."

And from another report: "Attendance was large beyond expectations.... Many can say, 'I have been anointed with fresh oil.' Even more noticeable is the blessing in the cases of many who have surrendered themselves to the Lord.... The good work is still proceeding quietly in our midst. We expect more blessing. The river of God is full of water!"

17

Made Perfect in Weakness

"Stop preaching at once!"

Such an order from Andrew's doctor must have come as a great shock and test to the untiring, fiery minister. During the constant preaching in his own church and on extended tours for special services for evangelism and missions, it was normal for him to speak several times a day. Often he traveled far into the night to reach the next destination.

"First I have to fulfill speaking engagements to which I am committed," argued Andrew.

"If you do, the condition will become far more serious. You will lose your voice altogether," insisted the doctor.

Because he did not immediately heed the warning, from 1879 he lost his voice for nearly two years. He was under strict orders to speak as little as possible and only in a whisper. He stayed for a time with his brother-in-law to escape the kind inquiries by visitors and to see if the dry Karroo air would help him while he was under the care of an able doctor there. The doctor treated his throat once a day, and twice each day for ten minutes he had to inhale steam with medicine mixed into it. He spent much of his time alone in his room or in the garden.

"The doctor says that he cannot say anything positive," wrote Andrew to his wife. "Not even whether there is any possibility of a cure.

I enjoy the quiet and have not yet found time hanging heavy upon me." He used his time to write regularly for a Christian magazine and produced tracts and booklets of a devotional nature. He made notes for the daily readings of the Bible and Prayer Union which he started. "With the cooperation of others, these notes may perhaps someday come to something." He added, "I have done a good deal of study and taken up the reading again of McCheyne's life with much profit."

Andrew could not stay away from certain conferences in Montagu and Worcester, where he was to have delivered important messages. These were read by someone else to the assembled brethren. He was unable to address the synod meeting in Cape Town as retiring moderator or take any active part, but they gave him a standing ovation of respect and gratitude for his services at that ceremony.

Why did God allow or ordain such a faithful servant as Andrew Murray to be set aside from preaching? The question must have been on the hearts if not on the lips of countless friends, co-workers and family. Andrew himself had been facing it in the depths of his own spirit. He was only fifty-one at the time.

He wrote to his wife, "My thoughts have been a good deal on the question of God's purpose for this long silence enforced upon me. You know what I have previously said about the two views of affliction: the one, that it is chastisement for sin; the other, that it is in the light of the kindness and love of God. I feel that it is a very great kindness to have such a time for the renewal of my bodily strength and of mental quiet and refreshment for the work before me.

"The thought has come, however, whether I might not be in danger of overlooking the former aspect. I have been asking the Lord to show me what specially there is that He wants changed in my life. The general answer is a very easy one, and yet it is difficult to realize at once distinctly where and how the change is to come. What is needed is a more spiritual life, more of the power of the Holy Ghost in my life first and then in my preaching. Yet it looks as if one's life is very much of a settled thing, and as if there is not much prospect of one's being lifted to a different platform. If the Holy Spirit were to come in great power to search and expose either my individual failings or the general low state of devotion in my soul, this would be the first step toward forsaking what is behind. Let us pray earnestly that our gracious God would search and try us and see whether there be any evil way in us."

During a visit to his childhood home at Graaff-Reinet, he stayed with his brother Charles. Charles apparently issued a brief medical bulletin to a Christian magazine that did not hint of any improvement in Andrew's condition. This worried Emma and the whole congregation at Wellington.

In comment, Andrew wrote his wife, "I'm sorry you were troubled about that notice, but it is simply the fact. . . . When people ask if I feel better, I never say yes, for I feel no difference. I have never written anything about being or feeling better. . . . I do not like to bother my doctor with questions about how long he thinks it may be until recovery."

Not long after that, Andrew reported that the doctor felt it would not be advisable to continue the silver nitrate treatments of his throat, suggesting rather that gentle and gradual exercise of the voice might be the next step. Gradually he might read or speak aloud in a room, later give short addresses, slowly uttered. That was good news and was followed later with his report that he preached for twenty-five minutes, and the doctor said it had done him no harm. A huskiness persisted that was expected to wear off. He had already spent nearly a year and a half in silence.

But the sovereign God had been working a perfect plan which did not allow for unexpected detours. While unable to speak, Andrew naturally turned to more intensive writing, for which he might not have found much time if he had continued in his ever-accelerating preaching schedule.

"I have been getting on quite nicely with my writing. Strange that I marked out the plan for a certain book some ten or twelve years ago, and now it is all at once flowing from my pen so easily. Writing makes me wonder at our slowness of growth." In the next few months he completed his new book in Dutch, the original of *Like Christ*, and issued his first venture in English, *Abide in Christ*, which previously was published in Dutch. "I feel a little nervous about my debut in English!" he remarked.

He gradually resumed his preaching and returned to Wellington to hold services during Pentecost for the concerns of missions, which lay so near to his heart. His congregation responded with a large sum for missions and for the Missionary Training Institute in gratitude to God for their pastor's restoration to health. However, the rejoicing was premature; Andrew suffered a considerable setback in his throat condition after that, so serious that he was advised to undertake a tour of Europe for a complete change of air and scene and to consult the best medical opinion there. Emma accompanied him.

Before his voyage God had already been working in Andrew's heart to consider the question of healing by faith. He read, though without any particular conviction, a book by an American, Dr. W. E. Boardman, titled *The Lord Thy Healer*. There were also certain meetings held in South Africa by a proponent of divine healing, and articles appeared in a Christian magazine by this minister, Rev. William Hazenberg.

Hazenberg's position was that diseases of believers must be regarded as judgments of God which God desires to remove instantly by believing prayers. His ideas were strongly challenged, especially his first assertion. However, many sincerely followed his teachings and he was in great demand in all parts of the country to lay hands upon the sick and pray for their recovery.

Andrew stated his beginning position in letters from Europe to his congregation, and continued to communicate with them how the Lord was leading him further as he inquired of God whether he did, indeed, have more to learn from the Word about God's perfect will for the health of His children.

"I had already given much thought to James 5:14–16 and together with others already made this matter of faith healing a subject of intercession. I had no doubt that the Lord even yet bestows healing on the prayer of faith. Yet it was as though I could not reach that level of faith. Facing this trip to Europe, I felt I had to make a critical decision: should I turn myself over to a doctor to treat me or should I turn *exclusively* to those who appear to have received this gift of healing from the Lord? I thought I'd made this decision while on board, but it was not settled."

Most of all, Andrew wanted to see Pastor Stockmaier whom he had met some years before, a truly spiritual man and at that time the head of an institute for faith healing in Switzerland. But he didn't expect to meet him until later.

Meanwhile, upon landing, he placed himself in the hands of a famous London physician who prescribed some medicines and treatment and continued consultation. A week later Andrew was to attend a Christian conference. To his surprise, Pastor Stockmaier was also present.

"I called on him and discussed my problem and my secret doubt that it may not be God's will that I should be healed. Rather, I countered, wouldn't it give God greater glory if I remained silent and served God in some other capacity? Surely sufferings and trials are means of grace which God uses to sanctify His people."

Pastor Stockmaier replied to Andrew, "You are still fettered by the customary views of suffering that most Christians hold. Observe how carefully James distinguishes in verses 13 and 14 between suffering and disease." He and Andrew diligently went over the exegesis of that passage, with the result that Andrew saw for himself clearly that there is no unconditional promise that suffering arising from the many temptations and trials of life would be taken away, nor should we pray to that end. There *is* such promise in the case of *sickness*, and *that* we should claim.

"I understand the matter better now. Suffering that comes upon the Christian from the world outside must serve to bless and sanctify him. But it is different with disease which has its origin within the body, not outside of it. The body has been redeemed. It is the temple of the Holy Spirit. For the believer who can accept it, the Lord is ready to reveal, even in the case of the body, His mighty power to deliver from the dominion of sin."

Pastor Stockmaier invited Andrew to attend the meetings of Dr. Boardman whose book about healing Andrew had read before coming to Europe. Dr. Boardman had written another book, *The Higher Christian Life*, and had opened an institute for faith healing called Bethshan. Because it was right in London, Andrew visited it and felt led to ask to be admitted as a patient. He remained in residence for three weeks.

"I imagine you may wonder why it was necessary to enter a special place and remain there for so long," Andrew wrote to his congregation. "You may think that surely the prayer of faith is a matter of a moment, just like the laying on of hands or the anointing with oil of which James speaks. Quite true. Yet in most cases, time is needed in order to learn what God's Word actually promises and to rightly understand what the cause and purpose of the disease really are, and what are the conditions and the meaning of healing. Remaining in such a home with all its surroundings helps to make this matter plain and to strengthen faith."

Andrew described their daily schedule: "Morning by morning sixteen or eighteen of us who sought healing gathered around the Word of God and were instructed as to what still remained in us to prevent us from appropriating the promise. We were taught what there was in Scripture to encourage us to faith and complete surrender. I cannot remember that I ever listened to expositions of the Word of God in which greater simplicity and a more glorious spirit of faith were revealed, combined with heart-searching application of God's demand to surrender everything to Him."

There were also times of private prayers and counseling with Pastor Stockmaier. "When he prayed with me the first time, he used the expression of 1 Corinthians 11:31–32, 'Lord, teach him to judge himself, that he may no longer be judged or chastened.' I find there the main thoughts concerning sickness and cure. In what way is sickness a chastisement? God judges us in love so that we may not be condemned with the world. If we judge ourselves in such a manner as to discover the reason for which we are being chastised, then, as soon as the reason is removed, the chastisement itself is no longer necessary. The disease was designed to bring us to complete severance from what God disapproves of in our life. When the Lord attains this purpose, He may remove the disease.

"Must these be specific sins, you may inquire? Sometimes, although not always. They may be a lack of complete consecration, the assertion of one's own will, confidence in one's own strength in performing the Lord's work, a forsaking of one's first love and tenderness in the walk with God, or the absence of that gentleness which desires to follow only the leading of the Spirit of God. . . . . Our surrender to the Holy Spirit as we ask for healing is to express our readiness to live every day in complete dependence upon the Lord for our bodily welfare. . . . The Lord, in thus giving and preserving health by faith, is really effecting the most intimate union with Himself."

Andrew made it clear that the believer who was healed was not to accept his healing and run, so to speak, considering it a once-for- all event and continue as before. He emphasized that a healing was meant to establish or reestablish a permanent, vital, ongoing moment-by-moment union with the Lord to maintain that new infusion of health.

Andrew knew whereof he spoke, for during his stay at the Bethshan Home, he was indeed *healed by the Lord* so completely that never again was he troubled by any weakness of throat or voice. He depended constantly upon the Lord for its use for the rest of his life. In spite of the heavy strain imposed on it, his voice retained its strength till his eighty-eighth year. The clear, youthful, musical, and penetrating quality surprised everyone. Those who heard him for the first time did not expect such a voice to issue from so frail and aged a body.

"Some object to, even shun, the possibility of healing because they think that disease and chastisement bring *blessing*. Do you not realize that recovery brings even *greater* blessing? When the healing brings about a closer contact with the living Lord and a more complete union of the body with Him, we can understand that such recovery does bring infinitely greater blessing to the soul than the disease could convey," he explained.

Before Andrew left South Africa, his state of health was so poor that a nephew wrote to his parents, "Uncle Andrew is very ill. You better come and say good-bye permanently to him before he goes to England." Andrew surprised everyone by returning to the ministry in full vigor. Not only so, but there was a noticeable change of manner in his dealings with people, an even deeper launching out into a walk in the Spirit, and a difference in tone in his preaching. God brought him through another sovereignly planned step of growth so that he might teach others.

His eldest daughter perceptively described the change in her father: "It was after the 'time of silence' when God came so near to father, and he saw even more clearly the meaning of a life of full surrender and simple faith, that in all his relationships he began to show a constant tenderness and unruffled loving-kindness and unselfish thought for others which increasingly characterized his life from that point. At the same time, he lost nothing of his strength and determination.

"More and more he expressed that wonderful, grave, and beautiful humility which could never be put on, but could only be the work of the indwelling Spirit. It was felt immediately by all who came into contact with him."

He had been serious and even severe during his overwhelming responsibilities in his youthful ministry in the Orange Free State and Transvaal. He dealt severely with himself and felt the need for strict discipline toward his people. This was in great contrast to his natural temperament, for when he first returned to South Africa straight from college, he was overflowing with fullness of life and merriment. But underneath he was always the same man, serious and yearning after the fullness of God, always surrendering himself more completely to his Lord, but maturing and mellowing as he became more attuned to the Spirit. God invested eighty-eight years to work into Andrew Murray the image and likeness of his adorable Master and Lord.

Photographs

circa 1866

Born in Scotland, Andrew Sr., progenitor of the Murray clan and father of the subject of this book, arrived at the cape in 1822. He was appointed minister at Graaff-Reinet where he served for 42 years.

circa 1875

Andrew Jr.'s parents had sixteen children, eleven of whom reached adulthood. Andrew's mother, Susanna, is in the center with the white cap. Andrew Jr. is seated at his mother's left shoulder in the photo. Andrew Sr. had already died when this picture was taken.

The parsonage at Graaff-Reinet, Andrew's birthplace.

Andrew as a seminary student in Holland.

Covered wagons and ox carts transported the newlywed Murrays.

Worcester during Andrew's pastorate.

Andrew as moderator of the Dutch Reformed Church.

Andrew's family, 1880.

"Clairvaux," the Murrays' Wellington home in their latter years. The veranda is where Andrew wrote many of his books.

Little Rolien Theron of Pretoria is fascinated by an old family photo album at Reinet House. (Courtesy of South African Panorama, September 1992)

18

The Afterward of Healing

Andrew's new faith in God's healing power was tested as soon as he arrived home. The Murrays left their younger children in the care of Miss McGill, an old friend of the family. She became seriously ill during their absence and met them with, "I have lived just long enough to deliver the children to you again."

"Oh, no," said Andrew. "God still needs you in South Africa, and He will restore you in answer to prayer. Though doctors despair, there is hope in the Lord who heals us." Then he explained to her the principles of faith healing and offered earnest prayer for her recovery. She was doubtful at first, but before long she stepped out on faith for her healing, regained strength, rose from her sick bed and with restored health labored many years in the Y.W.C.A. of Cape Town.

The subject of the Lord's healing was a vital part of Andrew's ministry from that point on. In 1884 he published in Dutch a book titled *Jesus, the Physician of the Sick.* He acknowledged that many objections may be leveled at faith healing to which no satisfactory answers can be found at present. But he stated that his aim was not so much to meet objections as to attempt an exposition of what Scripture taught on the subject. This book was later published in French and in English under the title *Divine Healing*, which Andrew much preferred. The connotations of the term "faith healing" might be construed to take in many philosophies which were not even Christian. But Andrew and those from whom he learned these truths understood and taught that it is *not faith* that heals, but faith is the hand that receives the gift from *the Healer, who is God.*

Let us ask Andrew more about his position on healing. (His answers are taken verbatim from his book *Divine Healing*.)

Were not the miracles and gifts of the Spirit only for the apostolic Church?

"Basing my views on Scripture, I do not believe that miracles and the other gifts of the Spirit were limited to the time of the primitive Church, nor that their object was to establish the foundation of Christianity and then disappear by God's withdrawal of them."

Why do we see them, including healing, so little today?

"Because the Church has become so worldly that the Spirit can act but feebly in her."

Can we expect to see more miracles today?

"If the Church were to see anew springing up within her, men and women who live the life of faith and of the Holy Spirit, entirely consecrated to their God, we would see again the manifestation of the same gifts as in former times. . . . The Church must expect great outpourings of the Spirit in these days, and may reckon upon this gift [of healing] likewise."

Is there any limitation to Mark 16:17–18 about the signs which Jesus said would follow those that believe?

"The Bible does not authorize us, either by the words of the Lord or His apostles, to believe that the gifts of healing were granted only to the early times of the Church. On the contrary, the promise of Jesus to the apostles when He gave them instructions shortly before His ascension concerning their mission appears to us *applicable to all times*. Paul places the gift of healing among the operations of the Holy Spirit. James gives a precise command on this matter *without restriction of time*. The entire Scriptures declare that these graces will be granted according to the measure of the Spirit and of faith."

Were not miracles much more necessary in the early days of Christianity than in our latter days?

"Ah no. What about the power of heathenism even today wherever the gospel seeks to combat it, even in our *modern* society, and in the midst of the ignorance and unbelief which reigns even in the Christian nations?"

"I had certain questions myself at the beginning of my search for God's truth in the matter of healing," admitted Andrew. One was: "Why, in many cases, is slow progress made with the healing process? If it is an act of God's almighty power, why is everyone not perfected *at once*?"

It was Dr. Boardman who helped him to a satisfactory answer. "Many times such gradual recovery brings about a learning to trust in the Lord and to continue in *constant* dependence upon Him. God is often educating His child to the increasing exercise of faith and to a continuance of communion with Himself."

Dr. Stockmaier reinforced this answer with his own experience of being wholly incapacitated from preaching for more than two years with a problem in his head. The trouble did not disappear even after he accepted the truth of healing, though he was always able to perform his work in the power of fellowship with the Lord by faith.

"He assured me," said Andrew, "that he would not for all the world have exchanged for an immediate recovery what he learned during two years of *gradual* healing.

"But I still had the question," wrote Andrew, "of whether an instantaneous and complete healing would not be a much more powerful proof, both for Christians and for the world at large, and bring more glory to God."

The answer which satisfied Andrew immediately was, "The Lord knows better than you what is for His greater glory. *Leave it to Him* to care for His own glory. Your duty is to hold fast to Him as your Healer, in whom you already have your healing, and He will enable you, in such manner as He sees fit, to perform all your work."

It is apparent from an interview between Andrew and one of his colleagues, Rev. J. R. Albertyn, that he never supported the assertion of some that "all disease has its source in the devil." He wrote that the sick were not more sinful than the sound. From his book *Divine*

Healing it is also apparent that he believed the divine mystery of the answer to prayer applied also to healing by faith.

Andrew had observed instantaneous healings, both while he was under instruction at Bethshan and in subsequent years through his own ministry. He held that God's sovereignty binds Him only to do His work perfectly with whatever variety He sees best.

"A girl at Bethshan suffered for years from many diseases, epilepsy among others, and several doctors declared nothing could be done for her. She lay half conscious on the sofa during the prayer meetings. Prayer continued on her behalf until one day when it seemed she suddenly grasped the full truth of Isaiah 53. She immediately rose and said, 'If Christ *has borne* my sicknesses, I need not *carry* them any longer.' Within a short time she was completely cured." Andrew declared that on subsequent occasions he heard her bear witness with great joy to the Lord's healing.

So convinced had Andrew become of the Lord's power to heal that he wondered "whether I may not perhaps possess the gift of healing and have the vocation and should devote myself, for a time at least, to this work. I notice in those who are engaged in this healing ministry that they must give almost all their time and strength to it so that their faith acquires sufficient vitality and strength to enable them to wrestle courageously with all the doubts and difficulties of their patients."

He consulted several mature Christian leaders who advised that *not everyone who had been healed* was to devote himself to the ministry of healing others. Each must wait for the Lord's guidance to assign his work according to his ability and God's plan. It was Samuel Zeller who reminded him that for some the ministry of the gospel might be a higher calling. At the same time, within the church and the leadership of the congregation, even among the ministers themselves, the gift of healing should be found very much more frequently as believers move more deeply in the Holy Spirit. Andrew found this remarkably true in the years to come as he ministered both the gospel and the healing teaching in the ordinary opportunities the Lord set before him.

Andrew apparently never receded from the position on divine healing to which he felt the Lord led him through the study of Scripture and his personal experience. It was not true that Andrew was henceforth never sick, weak, or without accident. Nor was it true that each case for which he prayed for healing recovered. There were some outstanding cases where much prayer was made and much faith exercised, and the believers still died. Several of his pastor friends and his own family members were among these, the young and dedicated as well as the old. Although Andrew did not understand why God did not heal in those cases and could not explain it to others, yet it did not shake his faith that God *can* and *does* and *will* heal, subject to His sovereignty, and that believers ought to obey Him and continue to ask in faith.

Did Andrew cease consulting doctors after he had found new faith in God as the Healer? To ease the minds of relatives and friends he did not refuse, as a rule, to see the doctor if they insisted.

"We may be thankful to God for giving us doctors," he wrote. "Their vocation is one of the most noble, and a large number of them seek truly to do with love and compassion all they can to alleviate the evils and sufferings which burden humanity as a result of sin. Some are zealous servants of Jesus Christ who also seek the good of their patients' souls.

"Nevertheless, it is Jesus Himself who is always the first, the best, the greatest Physician. Jesus heals diseases for which earthly physicians can do nothing. The Father gave Him this power when He charged Him with the work of our redemption. . . . Even in our day, how many have been given up by doctors as incurable, how many cases of cancer, infection, paralysis, heart disease, blindness, and deafness have been healed by Him! Is it not then astonishing that so small a number of the sick *apply to Him*?"

There were times, however, when Andrew felt he should cast himself upon the Great Physician alone. In 1907, already at an advanced age, he suffered from a severe attack of the flu, and it appeared he might die from it. His daughter described the situation: "Father was very ill and mother was quite brokenhearted and asked me, 'What am I to do?' I went to father and said, 'Father, dear, which will you do: have the doctor or have someone anoint you and pray with you?'

"Father said, 'I will have *neither*, my child. You can hold as many prayer meetings as you like, but *I will trust in God*!'

"I went out and arranged for three different meetings to pray for his restoration to health. To the praise of God, father, fully recovered, preached the next Sunday a most remarkable sermon on the text, 'They limited the Holy One of Israel' (Ps. 78:41). Once more father proved the faithfulness of God!"

When traveling in Natal on one of his evangelistic tours, the cart in which he was riding upset, he was thrown out, and his arm was visibly broken. He bandaged it himself as best he could, applied cold water compresses, and preached that evening as usual. The broken arm was made a matter of prayer, and so complete was the healing that some months later when Andrew showed it to a doctor friend, the doctor assured him that it was "most remarkably and perfectly set and healed."

Some years later, Andrew and Emma were both thrown from a cart on a similar tour into northern Transvaal, and he was seriously hurt in the leg and back. This time relatives insisted on calling a doctor, and though he did not give up his tour, he was never perfectly restored and had to forgo ever traveling by cart again.

His wife, like himself, was strongly convinced of the truth of divine healing and supported him in his ministry among the sick. Emma took suddenly ill and preceded him in death by eleven years. They had undoubtedly beseeched the Lord with earnest prayers of faith for her healing.

But neither Andrew nor Emma was unrealistic to think that there was no *natural end* to life on this earth. They recognized that earthly tabernacles do get worn out by use and time. God is preparing new bodies for His children, ready to be exchanged for their old ones, bodies which will last for all eternity.

And so it was that when his own fullness of time arrived to lay aside his tent of eighty-eight years, Andrew was not disappointed that he was not healed. He joyfully, peacefully accepted the providence of God and the timing of his promotion to Glory.

His daughter who cared for him in his last years commented that when the doctor ordered Andrew to be confined to bed, no patient was more obedient to instructions, more cheerful in attitude, or more grateful for the least attention.

She wrote about Andrew's attitude about not receiving healing from that cart accident: "One cool evening I was sitting with my father on the veranda, and he said to me in his humble way, 'My child, I would so much like to hold evangelistic meetings but God does not see fit to heal me.' He sighed a little as he said this, and I felt it was a mystery that at the very time God was using him so mightily as a soul-winner, this accident happened. But it proved to be his Peniel. He became, through that experience, a prince who prevailed with God in an even greater way in prayer. He was led through this seemingly strange providence into an even deeper prayer life and God taught him what the power of intercession really was."

His remarkable books on prayer were all written *after* that accident, and the influence they have exercised cannot be measured by man. God glorified Himself in His servant, and in spite of his lameness, he lived to a good old age. At last Andrew sweetly fell asleep in Jesus—"A shock of corn fully ripe."

19

Personal Testimony

"Why don't you write your autobiography, Mr. Murray, especially to trace your spiritual development?"

Many people of influence urged this upon him. Dr. Alexander Whyte was so intensely eager that Andrew should give to the world such a work that he said it would be the one book he wished to read before he died.

He even went so far as to send a note to his own publisher with a prospective title for Andrew's autobiography and attached the notation "In Preparation" on it. But to no avail.

Andrew maintained that his own spiritual experiences were not sufficiently clear-cut to instruct others by them. On one occasion his daughter brought up the subject again while Andrew was selecting quotations from William Law for one of his booklets.

"Well," he said, "if I could pass through Law's experiences, I might be persuaded to set down something, but not otherwise."

When she suggested that his own experiences had been equally deep and vivid, though not necessarily along the same lines as Law's, he shook his head and said, "No, my child. God has been very gracious to me, but in this matter I must have something more to go upon before I can venture to write." He persisted in this humble refusal to the end, and the world has no autobiography of Andrew Murray.

We must be content to trace his spiritual pilgrimage through the outward events of his life, his burdens and concerns, his preaching and teaching themes, and the topics of his writings. As we note the stages of Andrew's life in the foregoing, we glean something of his spiritual development. In this biography we have been observing successive changes and aspects of his increasing maturity. If we are alert, we can put the pieces together.

It is true, as Andrew declared, that his spiritual experiences were not really systematic and therefore should not be taken as a pattern for all believers. We will honor that. No one's life, no matter how prominent a Christian leader, should be taken as an ultimate pattern. All of God's children are still in process at any given period of their lives. God is continuing to work in them through their particular circumstances to shape them into the image of His Son.

Some have attempted a systematic study of Andrew Murray's theology, but the results have not been consistent. They have even been controversial in some respects—perhaps misunderstood. The question arises whether this does not bear witness to the depth of his teachings. Still less have his biographers succeeded in pinpointing the exact secret of his spiritual influence. Once again, this may be because of the inadequacy of any human standard by which to assess his life and work, or perhaps because his influence was like the atmosphere—essential and beneficial, but defying analysis and definition.

In this chapter we shall attempt to pick up some important pieces, heretofore missing, to round out as much as we can the portrayal of Andrew's spiritual development. Let us watch for the broad sweep and not stumble over details.

Andrew's manner of preaching was, from the beginning, very distinctive. Upon returning as a young preacher from Scotland, he was often asked to preach in his father's church. The sexton always asked to be alerted beforehand. "If Mr. Andrew preaches, I must remove the lamps on the pulpit table, for in his fiery zeal they will be in his way."

This characteristic marked his preaching throughout his life. Even in later years, some who heard him preach noted with interest the clouds of dust which rose from his pounding the pulpit cushion when he began his sermon. Before it was finished, they noted that the dusting was completed. Andrew was never violent or unrestrained, only glowing with desire to communicate and expressing intensity.

Despite his early zeal, Andrew was always spiritually discontented and reaching forward. "Ministerial responsibilities begin to press increasingly heavily upon me," he wrote early in his career. "Oh, how easy and content have I been living while souls have been perishing. How little have I felt the compassion with which Christ was moved when He wept over sinners. Oh! I feel it is not enough to be faithful in speaking the truth. The minister's spirit is something very different. Love to souls so filling our hearts that we cannot rest because of them would lead us to be very different from what we are. While I have been abundant in external labors, oh! yet I have felt nothing of that 'the zeal of thine house hath consumed me.' I trust that the Lord is, however, leading me to more earnestness in prayer, though I feel if He keep me not, my reluctant flesh is every moment ready to say, 'It is enough.'"

He wrote later, "Most cordially do I sympathize with Papa in the wishes he expresses for the Spirit to be granted in connection with our preaching. Yet, I do not know what hampers me so dreadfully in striving to believe in prayer or even to pray earnestly. I fear it is because my religion is as yet very much a selfish thing. . . . If my *own* soul be safe, or if *my* ministry be blessed, or if *our* church might be revived—this is too much yet the only motive in prayer. . . .

"As yet my prayers are not such as will draw down blessing. But it may be that God will give it of His great mercy. . . . I often enjoy much peace and happiness, but lest I should be exalted, the thorn in the flesh and the messenger of Satan is not wanting." Andrew pinpointed for us what he believed that thorn was: ". . . the fearful outbreak of my pride and self-esteem."

It seems that Andrew recognized the insidious danger of popularity and being well spoken of even in the context of the ministry. Everywhere he went he was acclaimed and praised. Even as a young man he realized that was not to his advantage.

"At moments I feel dissatisfied, then again very earnest, but still I fear there is at the root a secret feeling that I could be worse, and that there are many a great deal worse. . . .

"I thought I hated the name of being very diligent and earnest in the work of God, and yet my deceitful heart has not failed to appropriate a portion of the praise for the satisfaction of my own vanity. . . . I seem to have a secret self-complacency. . . . Why has the Lord put me in the ministry, so unfit as I am, leaving me to wrestle with the awful work in my own impotence? Oh! why can I not find the needful strength?"

In reflecting upon his condition later, he wrote, "I have thought much of the text, 'If ye abide in me, ye shall ask what ye will.' A man can't accomplish his work if his strength is not daily maintained by eating. So it is only a daily living on Christ that can make us strong for the great work of interceding for sinners. . . . Oh! for holier lives, more of the felt power of an indwelling Savior, more living participation in the new life and the power revealed in the resurrection of our Jesus." By allowing him to taste the lack of victorious living, God was seeding His servant Andrew for the writing of a simple book which has changed the lives of countless saints: *Abide in Christ.*

Andrew seldom gave what we would consider a personal testimony in his messages or in his writings. He remarked to a friend of the family once that some people objected to his reluctance. But that friend replied, "I think that the great power in your books consists of *just that*—there is so little of yourself in them, and Christ is always in the foreground."

"Mr. Murray, won't you make an exception and share just a *little* with us of your own spiritual pilgrimage from the beginning until now?" The request became insistent at a particular Keswick Convention in England. Andrew did make that exception by popular request, and shared, in much humility, some of God's dealings with him through the years. It was recorded in *The Christian* magazine of August 15, 1895. We consider it significant and precious because it is the only record of its kind. He was ever fearful of drawing the attention of his hearers from Christ to any experience.

> When I was asked to give my testimony, I doubted whether it would be desirable, and for this reason: we all know what helpfulness there

is in a clear-cut testimony of a man who can say: "There I was. I knelt down and God helped me, and I entered into the better life." I cannot give such a testimony, but I know what blessing it has often brought to me to read of such testimonies for the strengthening of my own faith. And yet I got this answer from those who urged me to speak: "Perhaps there are many at Keswick to whom a testimony concerning a life of more struggle and difficulty will be helpful." If it must be so, I replied, let me tell for the glory of God how He has led me.

Some of you have heard how I press upon you the *two* stages in the Christian life, and the step from the one to the other. The first ten years of my spiritual life were manifestly spent on the lower stage. I was a minister, I may say, as zealous and as earnest and as happy in my work as anyone, as far as love of the *work* was concerned. Yet all the time there was a burning in my heart, a dissatisfaction and restlessness inexpressible. What was the reason? Although my justification was as clear as noonday, and I knew the hour in which I received from God the joy of pardon, I had never learned, with all my theology, that *obedience* was possible.

I remember later in my little room at Bloemfontein how I used to sit and ask, What is the matter? Here I am, knowing that God has justified me in the blood of Christ, but I have *no power for service*. My thoughts, my words, my actions, my unfaithfulness—everything troubled me. Though all around thought me to be one of the most earnest of men, my life was one of deep dissatisfaction. I struggled and prayed as best I could.

One day I was talking with a missionary. I do not think that he knew much of the power of sanctification himself, and he would have admitted it. When we were talking and he saw my earnestness, he said, "Brother, remember that when God puts a desire into your heart, *He will fulfill it*." That helped me; I thought of it a hundred times. I want to say the same to you who are plunging about and struggling in the quagmire of helplessness and doubt. The desire that God puts into your heart He will fulfill.

If any are saying that God has not a place for them, let them trust God, and wait, and He will help you and show you what is your place. So the Lord led me until in His great mercy I had been eleven or twelve years in Bloemfontein. Then He brought me to another congregation in Worcester about the time when God's Holy Spirit was being poured out in America, Scotland, and Ireland. In 1860, when I had been six months in that congregation, God poured out His Spirit there in connection with my preaching, especially as I was moving about in the country, and a very unspeakable blessing came to me.

The first Dutch edition of my book *Abide in Christ* was written at that time. I would like you to understand that a minister or a Christian author may often be led to *say* more than he has *experienced*. I had *not* then experienced all that I wrote of. I cannot say that I experience it all perfectly even now.

Well, God helped me, and for seven or eight years I went on, always enquiring and seeking, and *always getting*. Then about 1870 came the great Holiness Movement. The letters that appeared in *The Revival* magazine touched my heart, and I was in close fellowship with what took place at Oxford and Brighton. It *all* helped me.

Perhaps if I were to talk of consecration, I might tell you of a certain evening there in my own study in Cape Town. Yet I cannot say that *that* was my deliverance, for I was still struggling. Later on my mind became much exercised about the baptism of the Holy Spirit, and I gave myself to God as perfectly as I could to receive the baptism of the Spirit. *Yet* there was failure. God forgive it. It was somehow as if I could not *get* what I wanted. Through all these stumblings God led me, without any very special experience that I can point to. But as I look back, I do believe now that He was giving me more and more of His blessed Spirit, had I but known it better.

I can help you more, perhaps, by speaking, not of any marked experience, but by telling very simply *what I think God has given me now*, in contrast to the first ten years of my Christian life.

In the first place, I have learned to place myself before God every day, as a vessel to be *filled* with His Holy Spirit. He has filled me with the blessed assurance that He, as the everlasting God, has guaranteed His own work in me. If there is one lesson that I am learning day by day, it is this: that it is *God who worketh all in all.* Oh, that I could help any brother or sister to realize this!

I was once preaching and a lady came to talk with me. She was a very pious woman, and I asked her, "How are you getting on?"

Her answer was, "Oh, just the way it always is, sometimes light and sometimes dark."

"My dear sister, where is *that* in the Bible?"

She said, "We have day and night in nature, and just so it is in our souls."

No, no! In the Bible we read, "Your sun shall no more go down." Let me believe that I am God's child, and that the Father in Christ, through the Holy Ghost, has set His love upon me, and that I may *abide* in His presence, not frequently, but *unceasingly*. The veil has been rent, the Holiest of all opened. By the grace of my God I have to take up my abode there, and there my God is going to teach me what I never could learn while I dwelt outside. My home is always in the abiding love of the Father in Heaven.

You will ask me, are you satisfied? Have you *got all* you want? God forbid! With the deepest feeling of my soul I can say *I am satisfied with Jesus now*. But there is also the consciousness of *how much fuller* the revelation can be of the exceeding abundance of His grace. Let us never hesitate to say, *This is only the beginning*. When we are brought into the Holiest of all, we are only beginning to take our right position with the Father.

I will tell you where you probably fail. You have never yet heartily believed that *He is working out your salvation*. Of course you believe that if a painter undertakes a picture, he must look to every shade and color and every touch upon the canvas. You believe that if a workman makes a table or a bench, he knows how to do his work. But you do *not* believe that the everlasting God is in the process of working out the image of His Son in you. As any sister here is doing a piece of ornamental or fancy work, following out the pattern in every detail, let her just think: "Can God not work out *in me* the purpose of His love?" If that piece of work is to be perfect, every stitch must be in its place. So remember that *not one minute* of your life should be *without God*. We often want God to come in at a certain time, say in the morning. Then we are content to live two or three hours on our own, and then He can come in again. No! God must be *every moment the Worker in your soul*.

It is no wonder, with a burning conviction like the above, that at those conventions Andrew was never weary of calling for the hymn with the refrain: "Moment by moment I'm kept in His love; Moment by moment I've life from above; Looking to Jesus till glory doth shine; Moment by moment, O Lord, I am Thine."

Andrew concluded his testimony:

May He teach us our own nothingness and transform us into the image of His Son and help us to go out to be a blessing to our fellow men. Let us trust Him and praise Him in the midst of a consciousness of failure and of a remaining tendency to sin. Notwithstanding this, let us believe that *our God loves to dwell in us*, and let us hope without ceasing in His *still more abundant* grace.

A further insight into the fact that Andrew was still pressing on, and was open to being taught by others, even while teaching others himself, is given in a letter to his sister. Apparently she wrote him that she wished she could consult with some of the key persons of the Holiness Movement, Mr. Robert Pearsall Smith or Dr. Boardman, to ask them what was the secret of their victory in the Christian life. Andrew answered that he felt he knew what they would say, as he had discussed that very point with them. He explained to his sister:

> Many felt as if the full baptism of the Spirit was lacking. The answers of these brethren all ran in one direction: You must trust Jesus in the assurance that He will make everything right *in due time*. You must really rest in Him as an all-sufficient portion. In your desires for more blessing, you must see that your joyful rest is not disturbed. The joyful, praising acknowledgment that you have everything in Him, that unutterable fullness *dwells* and that you *are* complete in Him must not be dimmed by the desire for what you do not *yet* see or feel.
>
> I spoke with a certain lady about it. She said we must remember that there is a diversity of gifts and operations in different people and at different times. Mrs. Hannah Whithall Smith was still seeking for a baptism of the Spirit while everybody thought she already had it and remarkably. It might be that we are mistaken in the idea we form of it. Experience, feeling, success are not given to all in the same degree.
>
> At Mr. Moody's after-meeting where I had been helping, speaking to the spiritually anxious, God sent an old man to deal with *us*. He said, "Brothers, may I ask whether *you* enjoy the full rest?"
>
> I gave an honest answer. In the course of conversation he said that such wishes may be a thought of the old nature leading me off from what I *am* in Christ—that I should say at once that I am dead to every thought of discontent and dissatisfaction. The Holy Spirit who *has* been given me *in His fullness* is equal to every need and emergency.

I spoke about it with Mr. and Mrs. Palmer who have for forty years been holding Holiness meetings in their own home in New York. Mr. Palmer said, "It may be a temptation of Satan. If you *have truly surrendered everything*, you must beware of being led off from your faith in Jesus by what you *still seek* in your experience." And we had a very precious prayer meeting together. And after a prayer meeting at Mrs. Keene's in Philadelphia, we had another talk. I spoke of the feeling I had that the blessing came more easily while in fellowship with other believers. She said that she had more than once attended Holiness meetings and seen people attain experiences of which *she* could not speak. Sometimes people who were not very well prepared or whose surrender was not so deep or full as that of others, apparently got less of a blessing. Her chief thought, too, was that we should *maintain the assurance of our surrender* and our trust, and *then ask and expect more* with patience.

See there, my dearest Ellen, what I have been taught in America—if not in the words of the speakers, yet in substance. And I have taken the lesson to myself and am rejoicing and will rejoice whatever comes, because *Jesus Christ, the Living Savior, is all I need!*

And you, too, should take this lesson and no more speak of the *feebleness* of your consecration. Our mistake is, I think, that *we form our own ideal* of an abiding exhibition of power and success which is *not* according to the mind of God. We *cannot* live so that *every* word we speak shall be blessed to the conversion of a soul, but we can live so that every word we speak shall be *to the glory of God*—spoken in quiet obedience and trust and then committed to Him who giveth the increase.

Interwoven in most of Andrew's teachings and writings is the concept of "holiness." It is important to know what position he took. He held that within the born-again Christian believer there does remain sinful tendency, but also held, as quite compatible with this, the possibility of a freedom from actual sinning. Holiness or perfection as applied to the believer does not mean that *we can no longer sin*, but that we are *able not to sin*.

Andrew defended it further: "It is a spiritual state which before death the sanctified can enter and remain there until death. It is entered by the blood of Jesus applied through specific faith and by one definite, marked, and well-remembered crisis. Different terms may be applied to it such as 'entire consecration,' or 'the baptism of the Spirit and fire,' or 'the fullness of faith,' etc. . . . God's plan is that soon after conversion, the sooner the better, we should enter into this Holiest of all."

The writer of one of Andrew's former biographies refers to a remarkable book, *Deeper Experiences of Famous Christians*, which documents accurately the experiences of Christians such as Madame Guyon, Fenelon, George Fox, Wesley, Whitefield, John Fletcher, Christmas Evans, William Bramwell, General Booth, Moody, A. J. Gordon, A. B. Earle, Frances Havergal and many others. Each of their testimonies includes a definite crisis experience they had *after their conversion*. It was as marked in time as a birth or a death or a marriage, and by it they passed into a new state and experience, a new relation to Christ and the Holy Spirit and a new appropriation and application of the all-cleansing power of the Blood, not only to cleanse but to keep clean.

Such witnesses are certainly considered illustrious and reliable. Andrew warned of the danger in thinking that such experiences are *exceptional* and that holiness is *optional*. He said that the possibility argues its necessity. The fact that it is *attainable* shows that it is *indispensable*.

20

Deeper Into Secrets

Did Andrew Murray feel that his teaching on the Holy Spirit was something new when viewed in the perspective of the historical Church and the finality of God's revelation in the Scriptures?

He explained it thus:

"It is generally admitted in the Church that the Holy Spirit has not the recognition which becomes Him as being the equal of the Father and the Son, the Divine Person through whom alone the Father and the Son can be truly possessed and known, in whom alone the Church has her beauty and her blessedness.

"In the Reformation, the gospel of Christ had to be vindicated from the terrible misapprehension which makes man's righteousness the ground of his acceptance, and the freeness of divine grace had to be maintained.

"To the ages that followed was committed the trust of building on that foundation and developing what the riches of grace would do for the believer through the indwelling of the Spirit of Jesus. The Church rested too content in what it received, and the teaching of all that the Holy Spirit will be to each believer in His guiding, sanctifying, strengthening power *has never yet taken the place it ought to have in our evangelical teaching and living.*"

Then he quoted from a book, *The Lord's Prayer* by Saphir: "If we review the history of the Church, we notice how many important truths clearly revealed already in Scripture have been allowed to *lie dormant for centuries*, unknown and unappreciated except by a few isolated Christians, until it pleased God to enlighten the Church by chosen witnesses and to bestow on His children the knowledge of hidden and forgotten treasures. For how long a period, even *after* the Reformation, were the doctrines of the *Holy Ghost*, His work in conversion, and His indwelling in the believer, *almost unknown!*"

God chose Andrew Murray as one of His spiritual miners to unearth some of the choicest of the "hidden and forgotten treasures" of the Holy Spirit to his generation, with the rich overflow to the generations that followed.

Andrew believed and taught: "There is such a thing as a Pentecost still, in the *personal experience* of the believer." The Holy Spirit, he believed, is the connecting and logical agent to undertake to communicate the holiness of Christ to us. The vital truth of the New Testament that the Christian is *holy in Christ* needs as its correlative that the *Holy One is in the Christian*. The outcome of personal holiness must be active service for Christ in saving men.

In answer to what is meant by the baptism of the Holy Ghost and whether it is not merely a part of our initial experience of the new birth when He comes to indwell us, Andrew explained:

"The baptism of the Holy Ghost is the crown and glory of Jesus' work, and we need it. We must *know* that we have it if we are to live the true Christian life. It is *more* than the Spirit's work in regeneration. It is the personal Spirit of Christ making Him present with us, always abiding in the heart in the power of His glorified nature. . . . To so many regenerate people this is only a blessing *registered* on their behalf but *not possessed* or *enjoyed*. It is the enduement with power to fill us with boldness in the presence of every danger, and to give the victory over every enemy.

"Whether we look upon this baptism as something we already have or something we must receive, in this we all agree: that it is only in the fellowship of Jesus, in faithful attachment and obedience to Him, that a baptized life can be *received* or *maintained* or *renewed*. . . . The question is, do we know Him as the *Baptizer* imparting the Holy Ghost or only as the *Atoner*, the Lamb of God taking away the sin of the world?"

Andrew was not indistinct or ambiguous in his theology of the Holy Spirit, but was anchored firmly in the full context of Scripture at every point. He stated his teaching clearly in many of his books but most specifically in *The Spirit of Christ* (even more in detail in the extensive notes comprising the last quarter of the book) and in his book *The Full Blessing of Pentecost*.

Drawing a few excerpts from the former book to spell out his convictions, we let Andrew speak:

> Every believer *has* the Holy Spirit dwelling in him. He ought to know this and believe that the Spirit will work in him what he needs for further growth and strength. The difference arises when the question comes to the *way* in which the believer is to *attain* the full experience of all that the indwelling of the Spirit implies.
>
> Two answers have been set forth: Believe that He is within you, open up and surrender your whole being to Him, and He will fill you. And the second: Wait before God for this filling as a special distinct gift, the fulfillment of the Father's promise. I do not believe that the Word of God teaches that *every* believer must consciously seek and receive, as a *distinct experience*, such a baptism. But I believe that it is in harmony with the teaching of Scripture that in answer to believing prayer, many believers *have* received, and those who seek it *will often receive*, such an inflow of the Spirit of God as will to them indeed be nothing less than a *new* baptism of the Spirit.
>
> Let us not fall into the extreme of saying that, since God has given and we have received the Spirit, we are no longer to *pray for more* of Him. It is often questioned, "But how can you ask for that which you already have?" Our lungs are full of breath, and yet call for a fresh supply every moment. Our fingers pulse with the fullness of blood, yet continually call to the heart for a fresh supply. . . . So our whole life of prayer should be the harmony of faith that praises for the Spirit that has been received, and yet always waits for His fuller inflow out of Him in whom all fullness dwells. . . .
>
> It would indeed be sad if a believer, on once having received the

Spirit, were to feel that the "how much more" of Jesus' promise was something he had now outgrown, and that this chief of blessings he need no longer ask for. No! As the anointing with fresh oil is a daily need, just so the thought of Jesus baptizing with the Spirit is not a remembrance of what is a *past* thing, done once for all, but a promise of what may and should be a daily, continuous experience. The faith that we have the Spirit within us, even when it has almost come like a new revelation, and filled us with joy and strength, *will lose* its freshness and its power *except* as the inflow is *maintained* in living fellowship with the Father and the Son.

Andrew summarized his own teachings in the following distilled statements:

> To the disciples, the baptism of the Spirit was very distinctly *not* His first bestowal for regeneration, but the definite communication of the presence in *power* of their glorified Lord.
>
> Of this Spirit, *every* believer is made a partaker. He *has* the Spirit of Christ dwelling in him.
>
> There may be, and in the great majority of Christians is, a contrast in their experience before and after the filling of the Spirit, just as was the state of the disciples before and after Pentecost. This difference, between the bare knowledge of His presence and the full revelation of the indwelling Christ in His glory, is due either to ignorance or unfaithfulness.
>
> When once the distinct recognition of what the indwelling of the Spirit was meant to *bring* is realized by the believer, and he is ready to give up all to partake of it, he may ask and expect what may be termed a baptism of the Spirit. He may receive such an inflow of the Holy Spirit as shall consciously lift him to a different level from the one on which he has hitherto lived.
>
> The *way* in which the baptism comes may be very different. To some it comes as a glad and sensible quickening of their spiritual life. They are so filled with the Spirit that all their *feelings* are stirred. They can speak of something they have distinctly *experienced* as a gift from the Father.
>
> To others it is given not to their feelings but to their *faith*. It comes as a deep, quiet, but clearer insight into the fullness of the Spirit in Christ as indeed being theirs, and a faith that feels confident

that His sufficiency is equal to every emergency that may arise. In the midst of weakness they know that the Power is resting on them. *In either case* they know that the blessing *has been given from above*, to be maintained in obedience and deep dependence on Him from whom it came.

Such a baptism is specially given as *power for work*. It may sometimes be received before the believer fully understands his calling to a ministry for others and while he is chiefly occupied with his own sanctification. But it cannot be maintained except as the call to *witness for the Lord* is obeyed.

The baptism at Pentecost and thereafter was distinctly given as preparation for witness. We must beware of laying down fixed rules [as to the manifestations of that baptism]. God's gifts and love are larger than our hearts.

Every believer who longs, up to the light that he has, to be fully surrendered to the glory of his Lord, may come and claim the fullness of the gift. It will prove its own power to *open the mouth* and bring forth testimony for God. . . . To some people, the fullness of the Holy Spirit may come without any idea of a baptism at all, but in intense devotion to their Lord, they *know* that He dwells in them and has them *wholly* as His own.

Andrew taught that the natural temperament of a person had something to do with the kind of response he or she has to the baptism or filling of the Holy Spirit. Also that the Holy Spirit sovereignly comes upon individuals and groups of believers in *different ways* at *different times*.

Those who received it variously are not to criticize those who differ, or discount their experiences as being unbiblical or invalid. He illustrated it beautifully from the South African scene with which he was most familiar:

> In our country where we often suffer from drought, we find two sorts of reservoirs for catching and storing water. On some farms you have a spring or well but with a stream too weak to irrigate with. There a reservoir is made for collecting the water, and the filling of the reservoir is the result of the gentle, quiet inflow from the fountain day and night.

In other cases, the farm has no spring and the reservoir is built in the bed of a stream or in a hollow where, when rain falls, water can be collected. In such a place, the filling of the reservoir with a heavy fall of rain is often the sudden work of a very few hours and is accompanied with a rush and violence not free from danger. The noiseless supply of the former farm is the surer because the supply, though apparently weaker, is permanent.

There is a similar difference in the way in which the fullness or baptism of the Spirit comes and also the response to it. On the day of Pentecost, or at times when new beginnings are made, or in the outpouring of the Spirit of conversion in heathen lands, or of revival among Christian people, suddenly, mightily, manifestly, men are filled with the Holy Ghost. In the enthusiasm and the joy of the newly-found salvation or revival, the power of the Spirit is *undeniably* present.

And yet, for those who receive it thus, there are special dangers. The blessing is often too much dependent on fellowship with others or extends only to the upper and more easily reached currents of the soul's life. The sudden is often, though not always, the superficial. The depths of the will and the inner life sometimes have not been reached.

There are other Christians who have never been partakers of any such marked experience and in whom, nevertheless, the fullness of the Spirit is no less distinctly seen in their deep and intense devotion to Jesus, in a walk in the light of His countenance and the consciousness of His holy presence, in the blamelessness of a life of simple trust and obedience, and in the humility of a self-sacrificing love to all.

Which of these is now the *true* way of being filled or baptized with the Spirit? The answer is easy. There are farms on which both the above-named reservoirs are to be found, auxiliary to each other. There are even reservoirs in which both the modes of filling are made use of. The regular, quiet, daily inflowing keeps them supplied in time of great drought; in time of rain they are ready to receive and store up large supplies.

There are some Christians who are not content unless they have special mighty visitations of the Spirit: the rushing mighty wind, floods outpoured, and the baptism of fire—these are their symbols.

There are others to whom the fountain springing up from within and quietly streaming forth appears to be the true type of the Spirit's work.

Happy are they who can *recognize God in both*, and hold themselves always ready to be blessed *in whichever way He comes*!

With such beautifully balanced Scriptural insights, it is no wonder that Andrew Murray spans the generations as a "mountaineer of the higher life"!

21

Missionary Statesman

Andrew Murray is best known for his ministry of the deeper life and the edification of believers, themes reflected in many of his writings. But his heart for missions was hardly equaled by any of the missionaries of his day or ours. From his childhood he met missionaries in the Graaff-Reinet parsonage and enjoyed firsthand opportunities to hear the great missionaries of his day while studying in Scotland and Holland as a young man. His passion was to reach all people for Christ—in his own country of Africa and wherever the waves washed on distant shores. He and his brother John were instrumental in establishing a student missionary group in Holland while in divinity school.

When Andrew began his ministry in South Africa in 1848, the modern missionary era was only half a century old. Up to that point, about a dozen or so missionary societies had begun work at the Cape.

Andrew's missionary vision always lay close to the surface of his call from God, and he sought every opportunity to fan it into flames in the church. At a meeting of the synod in Cape Town in 1857 some far-reaching decisions were made, among them that they should take a forward step in regard to mission work. A missionary committee was appointed, but its senior members were cautious and not very enthusiastic. They argued that their burden for the scattered *white* population in South Africa was already a heavy one and ministers were scarce anyway—one third of the churches were without pastors. How could they think of outreach to others?

The younger men, including the Murrays, were in touch with the missionary work of the ministers in Scotland and learned what God was doing in other countries. They also came into direct contact with thousands of tribal people in the Free State and Transvaal. They were eager to move forward, so a new committee was formed which represented the dawn of a new era in the Dutch Reformed Church and the beginning of its now widespread and successful missionary work.

For half a century Andrew continued to guide the mission policy of the Dutch Reformed Church. During the thirty years between 1886 and 1916, out of a total of some seventy who enlisted in the foreign missions program of the church, no less than twenty-one young men who were sons of ministers and missionaries entered the foreign mission field. Of this number fifteen belonged to the *Murray* family! Of Andrew's own children, his second daughter, Mary, and his sons John and Charles gave themselves to mission work.

As a result of the Worcester conference and the revival that followed, the missions impetus greatly increased, despite the fact that the Dutch Church in South Africa at that time numbered only fifty-three ministers. One of their initial burdens was for the tribal people of the Transvaal. Two of the ministers who were recruited from Europe, as has been mentioned, came specifically for missionary work. Andrew was asked to accompany them to the North and help make arrangements for starting the work. They were to be the first foreign missionaries of the Dutch Reformed Church to go beyond the boundary of the Colony and were the fruit of many prayers.

The journey was to be about a thousand miles, a difficult and time-consuming trip. Reaching Pretoria, Andrew had to confer with the members of the Executive Council resident at the capital. They were granted permission to begin missionary work, but only on one condition—that the consent of the tribal chief of the given district be secured beforehand. They didn't think that would be a problem, but they were stopped short by a resounding "No!" from a large gathering of some forty petty chiefs who were asked whether they would accept a teacher.

The missionaries were deeply tried and troubled by this setback and waited and prayed for a meeting with a second group of twelve chiefs. Again they received a rebuff. Andrew ultimately returned to Worcester, leaving the potential missionaries behind in language study. They patiently waited in quiet faith until it should please God to open the door—which was not until two years later.

Andrew wrote to his wife concerning the episode: "It was during these days of waiting that the thought of the blessing of the indwelling Spirit appeared so clear to me, the prospect of being filled with Him at moments so near that I could almost feel sure we would yet attain this happiness. The wretchedness of the uncertain life we mostly led, the certainty that it cannot be the Lord's pleasure to withhold from His bride the full communion of His love, the glorious prospect of what we could be and do if *truly filled* with the Spirit of God—all this combines to force one to be bold with God and say, 'I will not let Thee go except Thou bless me.'"

It appears that there was a deeper, more lasting experience of the fullness of the Holy Spirit that Andrew had not yet settled into. He felt a continued longing for still more of God's richness.

He wrote to Emma, "Yesterday I preached from the words 'Be filled with the Spirit,' and am only strengthened in the conviction that it is our calling just to take God's Word, setting forth what we are to be, as it stands, and seek and expect it, even though we cannot exactly comprehend what it means. In all the experience of the blessings of the gospel, the intellect must follow the heart and the life.

"We did not forget on Saturday evening that it was, if I calculate aright, the anniversary of the beginning of the great revival movement. May the Lord now grant us His Spirit, that all who believe may be filled with His grace and become entirely His."

Having to return without a mission accomplished in the sense that they hoped to establish foreign mission work immediately, was not a discouraging defeat to Andrew. He was learning many difficult but precious lessons of waiting, which eventually became the basis of his book *Waiting on God*. He wrote at that time, "I feel a quiet but strong confidence that the work is the Lord's and that, if I may say it, the responsibility of it is His."

Andrew's books were usually written in response to freshly personal and local needs, and in so doing he began to reach out to an ever larger circle of readers who identified with those needs.

In appealing to the churches on behalf of missions, Andrew wrote in a tract: "The Mission Committee has long spoken of extending the foreign missions work, but talking alone does not help. There are not enough laborers, and the work has been carried on for years with only three workers. Young men are not responding to be trained for the work. Thus it goes on year after year, and the heathen among whom we ought to labor are left in their darkness. The harvest is great and the laborers are few. The harvest is lost in the fields. Satan has no lack of men for saloon keepers, but the Lord Jesus seems to call in vain for missionaries!"

To meet the challenge he just pointed out, when Andrew accepted the Wellington pastorate he turned his hand to a closely related project—the establishment in 1877 of a boys' boarding home where missionaries and teachers might be trained.

Andrew was learning never to initiate any ministry, no matter how worthwhile it seemed to him and to others, "until quiet waiting upon God gave me the confidence to step out in faith on this new venture. . . . I feel that I have but one lesson to learn better, and I am learning it: just to sit and adore and say to Divine Grace that there is nothing I cannot expect His wondrous kindness to do."

He looked again to America for teachers and was successful in starting the work with ten boarders. It developed into the Missionary Training Institute which, as years went by, provided 145 ordained missionaries out of the 178 who were working in connection with the Dutch Reformed Church at a certain time. In 1905 this Institute passed into the hands of the Synod of the Dutch Reformed Church which carried it forward.

The uniqueness of the principles of this missionary institute was that it was established specifically for young men who sincerely wanted to work for the Lord but who did not have time, aptitude, or strong desire to pay much attention to intensive study of ancient languages or mathematics. The aim was to provide thorough biblical and general training so graduates could take their places in the church and in society both honorably and profitably. It also offered to men who were no longer in their early youth the chance of obtaining a good general education through the medium of both English and Dutch, and to do so at minimum cost and with adequate standard. It was, in essence, a Bible training school, rather than a seminary.

Andrew was always eager to encourage other Christian ministries, evangelistic services, missionary projects and specific works which the Lord had laid on the hearts of friends or strangers. It didn't matter whether they had any connection with his own church. To see the work of God's Kingdom go forward gave him the highest joy, and there was not a partisan feeling in his large heart. Whenever he heard of another young man's burden for some new outreach for the gospel, he would immediately pray with the brother, seek the Lord with him, and give him all the support that could be mustered from every direction. This was especially true of any Christian or group that was kindled for missions. Andrew was eager to help them launch their undertaking.

No estimate of Andrew's influence as a leader of missionary thought and enterprise would be complete that did not take into account his intimate connection with the South Africa General Mission. (It is known today as the Africa Evangelical Fellowship.) His interest dated from the time he met the twenty-three-year-old Spencer Walton at Keswick in England. The youth felt burdened for mission work in South Africa, and Andrew gave him every encouragement. Eventually Walton came to Cape Town to hold meetings with remarkable spiritual results, and the whole city was greatly stirred. Christians of every denomination were strengthened in their faith and stimulated to a life of greater consecration to Christ and to the service of their fellow men.

The Cape General Mission was established in 1889 with Andrew as president and Spencer Walton as director. From evangelism first among the white population who were leading irreligious and ungodly lives, primarily those who were beyond the reach of ordinary church effort, the mission quickly expanded to mission work among the tribal people in the fields unentered or insufficiently occupied. Swaziland, one of the neediest of South African fields, was soon entered and later other districts. In time The Cape General Mission absorbed the South-East Africa Evangelistic Mission and emerged as the South Africa General Mission with which Andrew continued to be deeply involved to the end of his life.

Mr. Walton and Andrew were also instrumental in inaugurating the annual convention at Wellington which became known as the South African Keswick.

When the general mission committee of the Cape church faced a serious deficit in 1908, Whitsunday (June 7) was proclaimed a day of prayer. In Wellington, Andrew, who was by then retired, delivered a powerful sermon on the text, "Speak unto the children of Israel that *they go forward*" (Exodus 14:15). Those who heard it could never forget it. Three days later the consistory decided to convene a conference on this matter in August. On that occasion the Laymen's Mission League was founded and £700 was pledged. After another series of mission conferences in which Andrew was involved, £10,000 was collected. Andrew inspired the movement and was the only one to attend all the conferences.

In his book *The Kingdom of God in South Africa* (1906) Andrew stated, "Prayer is the life of missions. Continual and believing prayer is the secret of the life-giving power and fruitfulness of mission work. The God of missions is the God of prayer."

22

Power for Outreach

Which of Andrew's many books was the most important or influential? In his day, as in succeeding generations of people who have been touched by his books, each person has a subjective favorite—one that has helped him most. The *South African Dictionary of National Biography* states:

> It is difficult to select a *magnum opus* from the list of Murray's publications. Perhaps it is because his works were so profoundly spiritual and therefore qualitatively equal. Yet his two major mission works, *The Key to the Missionary Problem* (1901) and *The State of the Church* (1911), with their Dutch translations, are conspicuous because they are by no means ordinary publications; they are events in the history of the Christian Church. Both works represented Murray's reaction to world missionary conferences: the Ecumenical Missionary Conference in New York in 1900 and the World Missionary Conference in Edinburgh in 1910. Both proved that he had a knack, more so than any other writer, to place his finger on the salient point or final issue and bring it to the notice of the world.

As an example of Andrew's impact upon his generation for the cause of missions, we will look more closely at the circumstances surrounding the writing of his most significant book on missions, *The Key to the Missionary Problem.*

"Andrew, what's in the telegram? The messenger boy said it was from New York."

Emerging from a baking task in the kitchen, wiping floured hands on her apron, Andrew's wife sat down on the veranda beside him. The year was 1899, and it was a special excitement to receive telegrams after having to wait months for letters to arrive by boat in previous years.

"It's an invitation to attend a missionary conference in New York next April, my dear. It will be the largest and most important ever held. They want me to speak."

"How can you go, Andrew?" Emma gazed thoughtfully and anxiously over the lawn and fields surrounding their home in Wellington. She knew her husband's thoughts would also be upon the Anglo-Boer War which had just broken out and in which so many of their fellow Christians and even family members were involved.

"No, I believe it would not be God's will for me to leave my people at this critical time. I am needed here now to pray and preach and give what counsel I can toward stopping this dreadful bloodshed among brethren." His face, lined with the spiritual concerns of fifty years of shepherding his people, nevertheless reflected a peace that could only be divinely imparted.

"You know how I feel about missions. I would so much like to be there. I will send them a telegram right away with my regrets and assure them of my prayers."

But the conference committee would not accept his refusal that easily because of his reputation and stature in the cause of missions. They followed with another more urgent invitation and a copy of the volume of agenda that had been issued in preparation for the conference so he might look it over.

Andrew searched his heart to be sure he understood God's leading not to go. "Do I have a message from the Lord for that meeting? Would I be able to give that message so clearly as to make it worthwhile to go all that distance? Would it be possible amid the great variety of subjects to secure the quiet, the time, and undivided attention for that which appears to me the one thing needful?"

The committee continued to approach him, this time through his friend, D. L. Moody. He too urged Andrew to come, and invited him to stay over after the conference and participate in Moody's meetings in Northfield. Nevertheless, Andrew still felt God did not want him to attend. All the while, the topics on the agenda and the great missionary issues involved were burning in his heart.

"My mind became clearer," he wrote, "and I felt that the one point on which I would have wished to speak was this: How the Church could be roused to know and do our Lord's will for the salvation of men." The omission of very important spiritual considerations in that preliminary report bothered Andrew.

"I received the impression that while very naturally the chief attention of the conference was directed to the work in the field, there was hardly notice given to the work at home and the fitting of the Church for doing its part faithfully. I felt that the basic issue was: There is no more spiritual and mysterious truth than that Christ our Head is actually and entirely dependent upon the members of His Body for carrying out the plans which He, as Head, has formed. It is only *spiritual* men, and a Church in which *spiritual* men have influence, that is capable of rightly carrying out Christ's commands. The clearest arguments, the most forcible appeals, avail little where this is not understood and aimed at as the true standard of Christian devotion."

Andrew felt strongly that no question was more urgent than: How is the Church to be reached and led to place herself, with every member and with all her powers, at her Lord's disposal for the work for which He has destined her and depends on her?

Not only had the preliminary report hardly alluded to any such point, but after the conference, when he received the two volumes of the proceedings, he spent hours eagerly going over every message, report, resolution and quotation to see if they had dealt with such foundational truths. While indirectly and implicitly it was admitted that there was something wrong with the greater part of professing Christians that hindered carrying out the missionary task, the real seriousness and sinfulness of the situation was *not* dealt with nor were recommendations made as to what the churches and missionary societies could do to change that. While acknowledging the many good things that came out of this landmark Ecumenical Missionary Conference, Andrew felt that the lack was so strategic that he should write a small book to that point, *The Key to the Missionary Problem.*

In its first chapter he prefaced his forthcoming weighty and sober words with:

> I know it is no easy task to humbly, wisely, lovingly and yet faithfully and effectually speak of what appears lacking or sinful in the Church. Yet I am sure that there are many who would welcome help in answering the question: Is there any prospect, any real possibility of such a revival in the Church that proof will be given that, as a whole, and in every congregation where the full gospel is preached, her only aim will be to carry the gospel to every creature? And if so, what is the path that will lead to this great change and what are the steps to be taken by those who lead the missions of the Church?

That little volume exploded upon the churches in America, Europe and South Africa in a way that perhaps a spoken message on the occasion of the conference, even by Andrew Murray, could never have done. As a result, we have in some more permanent form a summons to action for missions as burning and contemporary as it was more than a century ago. It was a book of great intensity which sounded a rousing and solemn call to new activity, fresh consecration, and more abundant prayer for the cause of missions.

The four principles on which he based the book were: that missions are the chief end of the Church; that the chief end of the ministry is to guide the Church in this work and fit her for it; that the chief end of preaching ought to be to train the congregation to take its part in helping the Church to fulfill her destiny; and that the chief end of every minister in this connection ought to be to seek grace to fit himself thoroughly for this work.

The keynote of this volume is: The missionary problem is a personal one; every believer is a soul-winner; every minister holds office under the Great Commission; the missionary enterprise is the work not merely of all but of each.

After dealing intelligently, knowledgeably, and deeply spiritually with important issues set in historical perspective and in the context of the Church worldwide, Andrew concluded the little volume with these burning words:

> Extraordinary circumstances require extraordinary measures. The discovery of an imminent danger justifies exceptional changes, and men willingly approve and submit to the inconvenience. The state of the Church, the need of the world, the command of Christ, appear to me to call for very special efforts. The urgency of the case is extreme. There is no time to be lost. Our Master wishes every human being without delay to know of His having come to the world to save him.
>
> Let not the enthusiasm of our watchword, "In This Generation!" deceive us. It may make us content that meantime the millions a year who are passing away in darkness should not know Him. It may deceive us with the idea that it is certainly going to be done. *But it is most certainly not going to be done if the Church remains at her present level.*
>
> The one deep impression the Report of the Conference leaves is that, unless pastors and members labor and pray with an entirely new devotion, the work cannot possibly be accomplished. It is so large, it is so difficult, it needs such an interposition of divine power, that, unless the Church returns to the pentecostal life of her first love, it cannot and will not be done!
>
> I say again, the urgency of the case is extreme. No sacrifice can be too great if we can only get the Church, or the most earnest part of it, to take time and wait unitedly before the Throne of God to review her position, to confess her shortcomings, to claim God's promise of power and to consecrate her all to His service.

The Key to the Missionary Problem produced an immediate and sober impression upon church and mission leaders throughout the Christian world and spread like wildfire through the ranks of the laymen.

Dr. Handley Moule, Bishop of Durham, England, wrote of it: "With all my heart I recommend this volume to the perusal, the thought and the prayers of all ministers of Christ and His flock. It is an appeal to the inmost soul of the pastor, and at the same time a suggestion for the most practical possible application of his activities. The great Christian who writes it puts his main propositions with an urgency which, just here and there, as it seems to me, invites the recollection of other sides of truth. His contention that the missionary enterprise of the Church is its supreme call seems, in places, to become the assertion that it is its *one* real call. But no deep-sighted reader will really mistake these places. And every reader who has indeed set his eyes toward the will of God will rise from the perusal, or rather kneel down after it, asking, 'Lord, what wouldst Thou have *me* to do?'"

Dr. R. F. Horton, of Hampstead, said: "Six weeks ago I brought Andrew Murray's book before my church and the people have bought and read about a hundred copies. I fervently trust that every *minister* will read it, for he makes clear that the key to the missionary problem is in the hand of the ministers. They open and no man can shut, they keep shut and no man can open. But I want the *people* to read it too because it seems to me the most inspiring and inspired book written in 1901—the true note of a new century."

With the same enthusiasm Dr. Alexander Maclaren wrote: "I hope that Mr. Murray's heart-searching book may be widely read and prayerfully pondered. It is '*The Key to the Missionary Problem*' indeed, but it is also the key to *most of our problems* and points to the only cure for all our weaknesses."

Dr. F. B. Meyer added his testimony in the following terms: "Of all the books that I have ever read on the call of our Lord to the evangelization of the world, this appeal by the beloved Andrew Murray must stand in the front rank, if not first. My heart has been deeply moved by it, and I propose to read large portions of it to my people. If it were only read universally throughout our churches by ministers and people alike, I believe it would lead to one of the greatest revivals of missionary enthusiasm the world has ever known!"

An anonymous letter in Dutch in the foremost Christian magazine of that day in South Africa echoed these impressions: "Next to the man who *writes* me a good book, I place the man who *recommends* a good book to me. A booklet came into my hands recently entitled *The Key to the Missionary Problem*. The writer is the well-known minister of Wellington. When I read it, I thanked the Lord for it, though it condemned me grievously. I also prayed that the Lord would direct its distribution and make its perusal a blessing to thousands. It will yield matter for addresses at missionary prayer meetings much more glowing than those of last month and the month before. Nor is it a book for the minister only but for all who take even a slight interest in the advancement of God's Kingdom. I know of no better means of kindling increased interest in the extension of that Kingdom than the circulation of this work. Followers of Jesus who read it and do not thereafter pray in a different manner to what they did before, must have a different spiritual constitution from that of the writer of these lines."

At the conclusion of his book, Andrew proposed that the subjects for the upcoming week of prayer, to be chosen by the Council of the Evangelical Alliance for January 1902, should deal exclusively with the relation of the Church to the Great Commission. Many regretted that this was never carried out but was modified to suggest that Christians should set aside a portion of time each day for the purpose of special intercession for missions.

Had Andrew's suggestion been followed, the writer of one of his biographies felt that there could be no doubt that a wonderful increase of missionary fervor throughout Christendom would have resulted. As it was, his proposal was adopted and carried out only in South Africa.

But there the results were striking. In the course of 1902 the Boer War ended. With the proclamation of peace, Boer prisoners who had been incarcerated in India and Ceylon, on St. Helens and on Bermuda, began to return from those various military camps. It turned out that more than 150 young men who accepted Christ as their Lord and Master in the camps now volunteered to go forth, after the necessary training, and *become missionaries among the peoples of Africa*. A special institution was founded for this purpose in 1903 called the Boer Missionary Institute at Worcester. It was the indirect result of the concentrated prayer to which the Dutch Reformed Church was roused through the influence of Andrew's book *The Key to the Missionary Problem*.

A reader of this book from Somersetshire just after its issue wrote, "I have been greatly profited by reading your book on missions. I cannot help thinking that some effort should be made to bring it to the notice of every member of the various churches. I respectfully suggest the issue of a million copies (to start with) at one penny each!"

Ed. Note: The author of this biography found a crumbling copy of Murray's book *The Key to the Missionary Problem*, and also Murray's important book *The State of the Church*, in the archives of a seminary while she was doing research. She discovered that neither had been reprinted in the United States. She contemporized their syntax somewhat, and Christian Literature Crusade published both, making them available for the first time to American readers in this generation.

23

An Anointed Pen

Andrew Murray had an inner compulsion to write. His spirit was too vast for the spoken word alone.

Andrew, did you ever imagine you would become a popular writer? we might ask him.

Surely he would laugh, with his easy sense of humor, and reply, "Certainly not, nor would I ever have believed that anyone beyond my rustic parish would be interested in my writing. But the Lord's hand became most evident upon it." Then, with a twinkle in his eye, "And Emma's hand, too. Without her fine literary background and enthusiasm for what I wanted to share, there would have been no books. Besides, with my permanently weak and shaky hand resulting from illness early in my life, I could not have held pen to paper long enough to write even one book."

His early writing was meant to be a simple help to the mothers of his flock, who, with their large families averaging a dozen or more children, had the main responsibility of teaching the first principles of Christianity to their children along with basic reading and writing skills. They were home schooling by necessity. Most of his wilderness congregation in the early years of his pastorate were scattered on lonely farms fifty or a hundred miles from Bloemfontein and rarely able to get to church.

What was your first book, Andrew, and how did you feel about it?

"My writing debut was in 1858 with a Life of Christ in the language of children which I had published in Europe. When I held that first precious copy in my hands, I exclaimed, 'I like it, but am disappointed that it is not more simple. There are passages that I hardly believe I myself have written!'"

Jesus, the Children's Friend, written originally in Dutch, was never translated into English because there were so many other good books of that nature in English. About this book Andrew commented to his brother John, "I was glad to see the advertisement of it. I would only wish my name left out of it. What do you think, from your experience, will be the time needed to get back the capital that has been laid out? You have never yet let me know what the printer's bill comes to. I would be sorry if you should suffer the least inconvenience in making my money arrangements. . . . Let me know, too, what impression the thing makes." Obviously, Andrew's books were self-published and self-financed. In the case of the first one, with his brother's help.

It may seem unusual that such a serious man as Andrew launched his writing career in the field of children's books. Yet not so strange when you remember that all his life he maintained a warm rapport with children and youth who took an immediate liking to him, feeling at home in his presence. His children's sermons were always popular. When away from home preaching in the early years, he would gather children around him at any opportunity and tell them a story or hear them recite their texts and hymns, and give them some to be learned for next time. Even at the age of eighty-six, he held the rapt attention of a congregation of some three hundred young people who listened to his explanation of the way of salvation. At the close of the three-day retreat it was touching to see over one hundred profess Christ.

"My second book likewise related to children, but it was for parents," Andrew explains. "It was titled *What Manner of Child Shall This Be?* The contents were mainly meditations and baptismal addresses for believing parents which I delivered during my early country travels. On some occasions I had to baptize forty or fifty children each Sunday. I tried to be careful not to do it *en masse* but give individual instruction to parents, even if the rite was administered in a tent, a tiny room, or farmhouse. I wrote this book as a guide for parents after I left." Later this book was published in English under the title *How to Raise Your Children for Christ*.

When he was already in his eighties and after retirement from his active pastorate, Andrew devoted even more time to the continuous writing of books and pamphlets. Whenever he would read something that stimulated his mind or spirit, he reached for his pen to see what the Lord would speak to him on some new aspect of divine truth from that spark.

In his earlier years, Emma took his dictation and was an eager sounding board for his ideas. His youngest daughter, Annie, acted as his actual writer during the latter years of his life. He would dictate for hours as Annie joyfully and patiently transcribed his thoughts.

One Good Friday morning as they returned from church, Andrew had some fresh thoughts which wouldn't wait until afternoon. "I must begin a new book right away," he insisted, and Annie was immediately pressed into taking down the titles of twenty chapters for a booklet on God's love.

Andrew's methods of writing were varied. Let's ask him about them.

Which come first, your titles or the chapter contents?

"Sometimes the one and sometimes the other," he confides. "But usually the outline is quite clear in my head first, then I can fill things in as the Lord reveals further thoughts to me."

Do you set aside certain times of the day for writing? we ask, in pursuit of some insight into his method of producing such a quantity of manuscripts.

"Sometimes I get home from conferences and meetings of considerable strain and weariness" (we don't wonder, Andrew, because you are in your eighties!), "but I must still hurry to write before the ideas flee. The other day I had to apologize to Annie that we had to write without her getting any rest. We did two chapters and eight chapter headings within a few hours.

"And then sometimes I don't sleep so well. The other night during the hours before dawn I composed in my mind three chapters of a little volume that I will call *Christ Our Life*."

Do you have an urge to write on certain topics, Andrew?

"Well, I sometimes put it this way," he replies with a chuckle, "I am like a hen about to lay an egg. I am restless and unhappy until I get the burden of the message off my mind. And when a book is finished, I like to have it quickly forwarded to the printer. But not before Annie and I pause and render unto the Lord a humble word of thanksgiving for His gracious guidance in the writing."

Would you share with us what you pray about your books?

"Lord, we have been endeavoring to instruct others. May we ourselves learn the truths Thou seekest to impart, and do Thou richly bless this book to all its readers. Amen."

Yes, Andrew, your prayers are still being answered more abundantly than you ever could have imagined. The glory belongs to the Lord, as you have wanted it.

Where did you get the idea for those handy carry-about booklets? Or were they an invention of some publisher?

"My nephew, Rev. A. A. Louw, visited me one day late in 1912 and drew from his pocket a tiny booklet written by someone else. I thought, how convenient for believers always to have such little books to carry and read at odd moments on the cart, in the train, at the railway station, anywhere and everywhere. And they would be good to give to others at little cost. I let no time elapse before I composed the first of such a series of my own works, which was *Lord, Teach Us To Pray*." (This book was later titled *The Secret of Intercession*.)

Twelve of these booklets came from Andrew's pen during the next five years, becoming the "Pocket Companion" series in English. Brief and to the point, these rich little booklets contain the cream of Andrew's teachings, written out of the ripe fullness of his experience in Christ.

What would you say are the characteristics of your style, Andrew?

"That is an unimportant subject to me," admits Andrew, "but apparently it interests others a great deal. I admire beauty and style in other writings, but I am very little concerned with my own. I lament that I have a miserable deficiency in composition. I have often said to Annie, 'My child, I have no style, or only a very bad style.' I have a burden on my heart from the Lord for that which I write, and I feel an urgency to deliver it and fulfill my solemn trust. Actually, the form which that message assumes is not a vital concern with me. When I was young and studying in Holland, I heard and read too much useless rhetoric from the pulpit and pen which was nothing but husks and stones without benefit to people. I want most of all to *feed* my people. The dish and tableware are not the direct means of nourishment!

"Many of my dear friends, however," he teases, "try to defend my style, or lack of it, by saying that I have bad English because I write in Dutch, and that I have bad Dutch because I think in English! Never mind. If God receives the glory and the sheep are fed, I am happy."

But thousands the world over do appreciate and admire Andrew Murray's style, the strength and eloquence born of deep earnestness and solemn issues which stir hearts and minds to spiritual heights and depths. The writings of Andrew are described as "moving the emotions, searching the conscience, and winnowing sins and shortcomings."

Annie, what are your father's writing habits? We are eager to glean every detail.

"Father sits up very straight in his study chair and dictates to me in a loud, clear voice, as though he were actually addressing his audience. His hours of work are usually from nine to eleven in the forenoon, during which two or three chapters of a book may be completed."

How about the punctuation, grammar, and general format of his books, Annie? Is that left to you?

"Oh, father is *very* particular about punctuation. And he always says, 'New paragraph,' pointing with his long, slender finger to the exact spot on my paper where the new line must begin. He says 'full-stop, comma, colon, semicolon' right where the sense would require. Should I make some mistake or spell something wrong, Father makes some playful remark like: 'Annie, you will have to go back to kindergarten, you know!'

"At eleven o'clock he says (when I myself am quite tired!), 'Now give me ten minutes rest—or no, let us write some letters for a change.' Then he quickly dictates half a dozen letters in reply to requests for prayer for healing, for the conversion of relatives, for deliverance of friends addicted to drink, or perhaps business letters. Occasionally he dictates letters for Christian magazines on the state of the Church, or for the newspaper or some matters affecting the country.

"Father always tucks the manuscript of a new book inside the pages of some magazine or journal for safekeeping. Then he will say, 'Now bring me *Father Christmas*,' and the manuscript pages of one of the "Pocket Companion" series is produced from within its covers, which had shielded the pages from being scattered."

Does your father stop writing when he is ill?

"If at all able, he keeps writing. When recovering, he always writes in bed. Even when weak, he dictates in a tone of great earnestness. And he has fussy ideas of how much writing I should get on a page. 'Write closer, closer,' he often repeats. When near the final page, he will say, 'Now the last four lines for a prayer.' Then he folds his hands, closes his eyes, and actually prays the prayer which ends the written meditation."

It is rather difficult to analyze the periods of Andrew's literary career too distinctly. He did pass through clearly defined stages of spiritual growth, and these can be traced in his writings, although his early books show remarkable maturity of thought and experience. In fact, all the teachings of his lifetime were present in embryo in some of his first major works, and they came forth one by one in greater intensity and depth as the years went by and his experiences increased. This emphasis is noticeable in the way Andrew underscored, had italicized, or printed in bold type certain words and sentences which he considered important in his books.

His first writings might be said to emphasize the *edification* of believers, their building up in faith and love and prayer. To this category belong *Abide in Christ, Like Christ, The New Life*, and others.

After 1888 the subject of *sanctification* gripped him, of which *Holy in Christ* is an example.

The final period may be characterized as stressing *intercessory prayer*, launched with *The State of the Church* in 1911. Still, the dividing lines are only vague and the subjects overlap.

Andrew was not a mystic in the sense of one who ignores the problems and hurts of his times. As the prophets of old, he never failed to speak out with insight and authority at critical moments in the history of his country, the Church, and the world. He raised his voice and his pen to direct attention to the real issues. He was said to "possess the gift of speaking at the right season, of having the right and just word, and of opening up the larger view and kindling the nobler emotions." This was echoed in his writings as he went beyond superficial symptoms to reach ultimate causes.

So universal were his teachings on the Christian faith that they leaped over ethnic and cultural barriers and were translated with equal profit into French, German, Italian, Spanish, Swedish, Danish, Russian, Yiddish, Arabic, Armenian, Telugu, Malaysian, Japanese and Chinese. A previous biographer stated, "Countless persons in every quarter of the globe hail Andrew Murray as their spiritual father, and ascribe whatever growth their Christian life has undergone to the influence of his priceless devotional works."

Did you make money on your book sales, Andrew?

"I was happy enough if I realized back the investment of publishing them! As for translations, my books frequently appeared in other languages even without my knowledge or my previous permission, so of course I got no financial profit from them. Neither did I want it. Whenever I was asked permission to allow a book to be translated, I freely and gladly gave it."

Do you know of specific instances in countries of totally different culture where your books have been a blessing in translation?

"Oh, many letters come to me, some written in foreign languages. For just one illustration, a missionary of the *Christian Literature Society for China* reported that when traveling in the interior of China, another missionary informed him of a striking discovery she had made. Apparently she had some of my books on her bookshelf but had not read them. One day she was led to do so and was filled with the Holy Spirit. The impact of that testimony led the journeying missionary to read my books also, and to translate *The Spirit of Christ* into Chinese. He informed me that it passed through many editions, and it was widely reported what spiritual good it had done among the Chinese Christians.

"He told me of one city where a revival broke out through that book in Chinese. In another case, a Chinese pastor preached on it

Sunday by Sunday, a chapter a week as a subject, and the church was tremendously revived. The prayer cycle at the end of my book *The Ministry of Intercession* was translated into Chinese and adapted to the Chinese church. *With Christ in the School of Prayer*, *Abide in Christ*, and several of my other books have likewise blessed the Chinese church, for which I do praise God."

Can you give us a particular instance when a certain piece of your writing arose from one of your life-situations and turned into a blessing for others?

"There are many. Almost all of my teachings and writings were motivated by experiences through which I passed. For a brief example then, when I visited England again in 1895, I suffered a recurrence of my back trouble resulting from the accident in Natal when I was thrown from a capsizing cart. I was to speak one evening at Exeter Hall and there was some doubt if I would be strong enough. Besides, through some misunderstanding of expressions I used in a message, which had given offense to some and provoked hostile criticisms, I would have been prone to be disturbed and distressed in mind. On top of that, when my hostess brought me breakfast, she informed me of a person who was seeking my counsel and was in great trouble.

"'Well, just give her this paper which I have been writing for my own edification. It may be that she will find it helpful,' I said on that occasion. It happened that my little message of assurance to myself of God's appointment in my time of adversity was so appreciated by my friends that they had it printed on cards and distributed in large quantities."

Please do repeat it for us!
"Very well:

IN TIME OF TROUBLE SAY:
First—
God brought me here. It is by His will I am in this strait place. In that I will rest.

Next—
He will keep me in His love and give me grace in this trial to behave as His child.

Then—
He will make the trial a blessing, teaching me the lessons He intends me to learn, and working in me the grace He means to bestow.

Last—
In His good time He can bring me out again—how and when He knows.

Say: I am here—
1. By God's appointment.
2. In His keeping.
3. Under His training.
4. For His time.

Psalm 50:15

Usually writers are wide readers of other people's books. Are you? And which books or authors have significantly influenced your life?
"In my student years, certainly I did much reading. In my uncle's home in Scotland I was thrown into a great reading atmosphere because the manse was well supplied with church magazines, missionary periodicals, theological and devotional books, and works of general literature. Missionary biographies were my particular favorites. During the years of our marriage, Emma and I read together on a regular basis, or I asked her to read to me as I relaxed after meetings. She was a cultured and well-read lady from her youth and kept bringing the importance of reading before me, which delight we shared together in spite of the ceaseless activity of our growing and spirited family. I have always kept in touch through periodicals with what is going on in the Christian world at large, as well as the matters of the nations."

"Novels he will *not* read," adds Annie. "But biographies are father's delight. His bookshelves are crowded with works in the educational as well as the religious field. Some of his favorites are those of Fox, Brainerd, Wesley, Burns, Bonar, Müller, Moody, and Hudson Taylor."

Never wanting to keep to himself his discoveries from the reading of good books, Andrew regularly would read aloud to his family at mealtimes the passages which struck him as memorable. He heard this done in his childhood home, again in his uncle's manse in Scotland, and he perpetuated it in his own family circle with great profit to all. He habitually wrote quotations and moral axioms on little cards for future use. One that he wrote on a shop ticket taken from his dressing gown was, "Live in that which should be, and you will transform that which is."

Andrew, you must have some particular interest in William Law since you edited selections from several of his books. Who was he and why do you feel he was significant?

"Law was born in 1686, an English clergyman who studied at and then was a fellow at Cambridge. But owing to his refusal to take the oath of allegiance to George I, he lost his position there and was, in effect, blacklisted by the state church. The subsequent enforced inactivity proved to be the doorway into a life of meditation and prayer.

"Law's life was greatly influenced by the works of Jacob Boehme, who taught him that which he had only faintly seen before, that God not only *is all*, and must *have all*, but that He alone must *do all*. He wrote on the nature and practice of intimacy with God. The more I read of his writings, the more I am impressed by his insight, range, and power. To share Law's spiritual depths with other Christians in a more readable way, I have edited selections from some of his books."

But Andrew, wasn't Law a controversial figure? Even unorthodox in very basic doctrines?

"Law did, indeed, represent the mysticism of his period which carried with it certain non-evangelical conclusions. Both Jacob Boehme, who influenced the later years and philosophy of Law, and Law himself, were unorthodox in many of their tenets. I am aware of these problems and have written a clear word of explanation to the Christian public. But it is because I believe Law's teachings supply what many are looking for, that I venture to recommend them. I do so in the confidence that no one will think that I have done so because I consider the truths that he denies are matters of minor importance, or that I have any sympathy with his erroneous views. . . . It often happens that where one side of the truth has laid powerful hold, another aspect has been neglected or denied. This was markedly the case with William Law."

It is enough to say that Andrew Murray, while laying stress on the supreme and positive message of mysticism—the necessity for union with the Divine—avoided the errors to which it is prone. His training in evangelical and reformed theology was so thorough, and his study of Scripture so excellent and continuous, as to keep him from going astray into the byways of mystical speculation. Andrew's own intense interest in mysticism he ascribed mainly to J. T. Beck, the German theologian. But the medieval Jan van Ruusbroec, Madame Guyon, Count Zinzendorf, and the other German Pietists also influenced Andrew.

The three books that are currently in print of Murray's editing of William Law's works are *Wholly for God*, *Freedom From a Self-Centered Life*, and *The Power of the Spirit*. Andrew sought to help some readers who might not be able to take in Law's teachings firsthand or have opportunity to study them thoroughly to see what his main points were.

Andrew, do you feel that you yourself must fully understand and live out every topic you write about?

"It often happens that after I have spoken in a conference or even after I have written a book, it is only then I begin to see the importance and meaning of the truth with which I have been occupied. Later, some of the very vital truths I have set forth come home to my own heart with special power as I apply them to new situations in my life or in the teaching of others."

"I remember," adds Annie, "when Father was preparing for bed one night recently, I saw a copy of his own book, *The State of the Church*, under his arm. Drawing it out, he said, 'Many a minister or other friend has said to me that he has read this book. Yes, they have read it through and then put it on their study shelves among other books they have completed. Now I wrote this book myself, and yet I have to re-read it so I may be able to take in the true state of the Church and be suitably moved by it.'"

Do you have some counsel, Andrew, for those who read your books?

"Yes. The disposition of mind is very important. My books should not be read quickly or superficially or only once. They are to be meditated upon to gain the fullest nourishment. More than that, it is not enough that the reader should understand and appropriate my thoughts, and then rejoice because of some new insight he has obtained, or stop with the pleasure which that knowledge has brought. There is something else. He must surrender himself to the truth so that he shall be ready, with an undivided will, *immediately to perform all* that he shall learn to be God's will.

"I would suggest that the reader verbalize it this way: 'What God says, I will do. And if I see that anything is according to His will, I will immediately receive it and act upon it.'"

Annie, was there any book your father wanted to write but never did?

"Oh yes, one especially. He had been gathering resource books, some of them in German, on the topic for many years. He earnestly hoped to write on the outpouring of the Holy Spirit upon the Moravians in 1727 and its relation to missions in connection with the life of Count Zinzendorf. But he was not able to do so before the Lord promoted him to Glory."

Thank you, Andrew, for obeying God's leading to write. You left us so many books to draw us on, generation after generation, to the deeper, higher life in Christ. And thank you, Emma and Annie, for being hands for him so that he could express his great heart in print.

24

Ripening Years—Climbing Higher

"What if we can't get along?" hesitatingly asked the appointee associate-pastor, Rev. J. R. Albertyn, before accepting a position as the colleague of such a well-known minister as Andrew.

"Come along, my brother," replied Andrew. "I will agree with you. Only be sure you are always right!"

The two became close friends in the Wellington pastorate and Andrew was freed for a great deal more travel for evangelistic services. The Murrays vacated the parsonage and built their own home on a most beautiful site nearby. They called it "Clairvaux" after the famous abbey which Bernard of Clairvaux founded on the plains of Champagne. It continued to be a hub of hospitality to everyone until the end of Andrew's life.

Mealtimes, especially, were times when everyone from the oldest to the youngest who lived under the Murray roof gathered not only for food for the body but for fellowship and spiritual sharing. One guest commented, "Meals with the Murrays are like Holy Communion."

On the occasion of Andrew's seventieth birthday, 1898, his ministerial jubilee was also celebrated. For almost a week there were celebrations in his church and in all the schools and missions with which he was involved. His old university in Aberdeen conferred on him the honorary degree of D.D. (Later, in 1907, he was awarded a D. Lit. from the University of the Cape of Good Hope.) In recognition of the 1,000 teachers who had been sent out from the Huguenot Seminary which Andrew founded, £1,000 was raised as a special birthday gift for Andrew for the school.

For nearly a quarter of a century, Andrew had been reelected as moderator of his church, the highest office, for which he was uniquely gifted. He knew the strength and weakness of his church, and his initiative and persistent energy were enough to carry through his purposes. His business ability, insight into the basic truth of any matter, and his knowledge of church law, gave him almost unerring judgment. He knew human nature and how to intervene in a debate at the right psychological moment, while his ready wit and humor often cleared a highly charged atmosphere of dangerous elements. He was firm without being obstinate, tolerant without being weak, impartial without being irresolute. He was courteous, tactful in public, and readily accessible in private.

Andrew was active in the Ministers Association, and even when well over seventy, rose to catch the 6:15 morning train to Cape Town for its monthly breakfast and conference. "The lesson I have learned after a half century of ministerial work is that God has for every man a sphere of work and a plan of work. The more unreservedly a man submits to God's will, the more completely God's work is carried out."

Emma did worry about him when he undertook strenuous trips in the Free State for evangelistic work because he threw himself so energetically into it. She wrote to her family, "I fear sometimes that Andrew will be laid to rest in that country of his first love . . . but I have ceased to be anxious about him and only trust God. It is He who gives him strength and will give it as long as He sees best. But some have remarked that when he is gone, six ministers will not be able to do his work. He is just head over ears in *missions* and what can be done to rouse the Church to its calling to live for the Kingdom of God."

When the Anglo-Boer war broke out in 1899, Andrew and his family suffered much heart anguish because of friends and relatives on both sides. Many of his old friends turned away from him, some criticizing that he was too pro-Boer and others that he was too pro-British. There were church leaders on both sides, but they would not heed Andrew's call to come together in prayer. Andrew reached out in spiritual concern to the prisoners of war in the camps, tried to find chaplains acceptable to both sides, and took charge of many services himself. The Lord moved mightily among the men in these camps, and many were converted. One hundred and fifty of them, as we noted, actually entered missionary training institutions at the conclusion of the war.

The strain of the war affected Andrew keenly and his health deteriorated. With his wife and two daughters, he spent some time in Switzerland to recuperate and devote quiet time in prayer. After peace was declared, the Murrays returned home.

In 1905 Emma was suddenly promoted to Glory, apparently suffering a stroke. The severing of their happy union of nearly fifty years was a heavy blow to the aging Andrew, though his immediate prayer of thanksgiving to God after her passing lifted the family to the gates of Heaven. He preached as usual the following Sunday, using the text "With Christ, which is far better." He threw himself into work for the Lord so strenuously that he also had a slight stroke which kept him in bed for some weeks. This situation precipitated his decision to retire from the responsibility of being in charge of a congregation. So, after fifty-seven years in the ministry, he became Pastor Emeritus, continuing to live at Clairvaux.

But the Lord had a still wider ministry for His servant for the remaining twelve years of his life when he became closely involved in the "Keswick Convention" ministries.

That which became known as "Keswick" teaching had, in fact, been a part of Andrew's inner experience and spiritual lifestyle throughout most of his life. Because it was said that Emma's spiritual life mirrored that of her husband most beautifully, Emma's record of the essence of that teaching is valuable:

> There is a step higher than just looking forward to Heaven. We may have our life so in Christ that even here below we may enjoy peace and happiness in Him which no earthly events can shake or destroy. And it is not by despising or trampling upon earthly things, but *living above*

them, willing and loving to live for His glory and the good of others, and counting it all joy even in tribulation for His sake.

God means us to know and experience that perfect peace and quiet of mind under all circumstances *is possible*. Nothing interferes more with work or renders it more difficult than fretting or worrying. In such a state of mind we can do nothing well. We must in a childlike way acknowledge God's will in everything with His peace in our hearts and a truly humble walk with God, bowing to His will. . . .

All this is attainable through the *indwelling of the Holy Spirit* of God, through receiving Christ as our Sanctification as well as our Justification. It is through an entire, unconditional surrender of ourselves to Him and an entire cessation from our own efforts and works, while waiting for the suggestions and influences of the Holy Spirit. And through believing in His indwelling and expecting His guidance even in the minutest concerns of our daily life.

Andrew kept closely in touch with the great spiritual movements of the world through reading books by their leaders and listening to reports of friends who had been involved with conferences. The Holiness Movement began in America and England, and many Christians were stirred to live deeper spiritual lives. The writings of Dr. Boardman, Dr. Cullus, Hudson Taylor, and George Müller echoed in Andrew's spiritual life.

One of his biographers described his development: "A profound though quietly wrought change was taking place in Mr. Murray. A born ruler of men, he nevertheless sought and obtained from God, from this point forward, a remarkable measure of the meekness and gentleness of Christ. It was wonderful how these qualities, united with humility and patience, marked the following years without any loss of strength."

Andrew prayed from that time on "to be made a fountain of love to all around," and it was evident to all that this was a special mark of the Lord upon him. "It is no new Christ or Christology, but Christ in a new and nearer aspect. It is an open secret to those whom God teaches," Andrew explained.

In due time Andrew came to be recognized as one of the leading Holiness teachers of the world, and invitations to minister in conferences were many. In 1895 he went to England at the invitation of the Keswick Convention. Situated in England's famous Lake District, this convention was known throughout the Christian world for its annual conferences to promote greater spiritual intensity. Andrew's addresses were full of power and fire in spite of the fact that his physical appearance was worn and weak. "One feels the presence of Christ whenever with him," was the continuous comment.

Describing Andrew's effect upon the Keswick audiences, Rev. Evan H. Hopkins, father of the Keswick movement in England, related, "His addresses came home to so many with peculiar power... it seemed as if none could escape, as if none could choose but to let Christ Himself, in the power of His living Spirit, be the One to live, although the cost was our taking the place of death.... As Mr. Murray dwelt on this more and more deeply as the days went on, especially at the solemn evening meetings, there came over some of us a memory of the early days of Keswick when an awe of God fell upon the whole assembly in a way that the writer has never seen equaled."

Andrew went to America immediately afterward to the Northfield Convention at the urgent invitation of D. L. Moody. For two weeks Andrew conducted the morning sessions with one theme totally absorbing him: the feeble and sickly religious life of the Church. In addition to the general public, four hundred ministers, including Mr. Moody and Dr. A. T. Pierson, attended those meetings and testified to great blessing from Andrew's preaching. Dr. Pierson joined Andrew in conventions at Toronto, Boston, Chicago, New York and elsewhere. He testified to taking a new step of consecration at Andrew's meetings, after which his deepened spiritual life led him to lay somewhat less emphasis on the work of foreign missions and more on the Spirit of Christ *in all* of life and service.

Andrew's observation from his North American travels was: "The spiritual life of the pulpit has not struck us so much as that of the home and the individual. As in England, the pulpit aims too much after literary culture and cannot get this without paying a heavy price for it—the 'wisdom of words making the cross of none effect.'"

Crossing back over to Holland for a remarkable series of meetings, Andrew addressed a crowd of over two thousand people from the very pulpit of the Cathedral at Utrecht before which, at his confirmation fifty years before, he first made public profession of his faith in Christ. In more than a half dozen other Dutch cities, crowds flocked to his services and an awakening of deep spiritual dimensions ensued.

He moved on to Ireland and Scotland before returning to London for a large Spiritual Life Convention where he made seven speeches within three days, delivering his discourses as usual without using manuscript or notes. His specific message was "Let us sooner and more completely not only believe in but have a full realization of our completeness in Christ Jesus." And again, "You must learn to know and trust Omnipotence. Let us make God's omnipotence the measure of our *expectation*. . . . We must take God at His word and return to the rapture and fire of the first apostleship. . . . God will put no difference between the Church of that time and ours in the results that He will give us to reap."

For the last twenty-eight years of his life, Andrew was considered the father of the Keswick movement in South Africa. Patterned along the lines of the English Keswick Convention, its teachings were generally about whole-hearted consecration to God. Speakers proclaimed the possibility of a child of God being so filled with and led by the Holy Spirit that a life well-pleasing to God may be lived here on earth. Andrew became the president and chairman of the South African Keswick and continued as such until his death.

Basic topics of the Convention were: the necessity of entire surrender to the Lord; complete cleansing from sin through the precious Blood; and the fullness and anointing of the Holy Spirit for life and service.

The results of the annual conferences were far reaching upon the Church of Christ in South Africa. Many of the outstanding workers in the different churches and missions, both ministers and laymen who were used mightily by God, received their inspiration and spiritual equipment in these gatherings.

One of the outstanding features of these Keswicks was the number who entered into a very definite experience of the fullness or baptism of the Holy Spirit and reached a place of real victory and power over sin. Andrew insisted that the speakers be very clear-cut in their teaching and was careful to invite only those who fully concurred with the Convention position.

Because travel remained difficult and time-consuming, by popular demand arrangements were made for the holding of similar but separate conferences in more than a half dozen other South African towns. Andrew always tried to work in harmony with the ministers of the various churches in any region. Not all accepted his spiritual teaching platform, but their relationships were open and brotherly. One of the most argumentative and perhaps least sympathetic of the local ministers in a certain place spoke out: "Well, I do not accept Mr. Murray's teaching, but one is left in no doubt as to *what* he teaches. It is clear as daylight!"

One of Andrew's Keswick messages on the subject of the filling of the Holy Spirit is typical, revealing his clarity and boldness of teaching. His main points were:

"I *must* be filled. It is absolutely *necessary*.

I *may* be filled. God has made it blessedly *possible*.

I *would* be filled. It is eminently *desirable*.

I *will* be filled. It is so blessedly *certain*."

Andrew's message was always simple: Come to Jesus; abide in Him; work through Him. Repeatedly he emphasized the little central word "in." "The two parts of the promise 'Abide *in* me and I *in* you' find their union in that significant little word. There is no more profound word in all of Scripture," he declared.

In the last years of his life, Andrew became quite deaf but remarkably continued to be chairman of the Keswick Convention. He kept in touch with the proceedings by asking someone to give him running notes of the addresses.

The most active evangelistic outreach years of Andrew's ministry were from 1879 to 1891. Seven evangelistic campaigns were held in scattered parts of South Africa with Andrew as speaker. His congregation acknowledged his special gift and calling for evangelism and gladly granted him leave of absence for those revivals.

To understand how he could conduct such extensive campaigns without any modern equipment, easy transportation, or professional staff, which our age seems to consider essential, let us ask Andrew:

How do you get ready for such meetings when you are invited to a certain church?

"I instruct the minister of the congregation how best to kindle large expectations of what God is going to do in their midst. It is important that the audience be spiritually ripe to receive God's truth. I want him to urge believers to pray continuously and in faith not only for a general blessing, but for individuals whom God has laid on their hearts—family members and friends. At the same time, I enlist the prayer of other congregations in churches at large to bear up each evangelistic service in their intercession, so that it might please God to grant a rich harvest of souls."

Does someone else take care of all your travel arrangements so you may devote yourself fully to the ministry?

"No, I usually attend to the details of travel myself, both the stages of my itinerary and all the meeting schedules."

Does everyone welcome such meetings?

"Ah, no. There are prejudices to be removed, difficulties to be smoothed away, ignorance to be dispelled, and coldness and diffidence to be overcome."

What particular objections might a minister have regarding a revival?

"Some are not against special services as such, but they fear the 'after-meetings.' We are a very formal and ordered people in the Dutch Church. But I have learned from my friend D. L. Moody that these are absolutely essential to conserve the spiritual results and to strengthen the new babies. I tell them that it would be like breaking off the point of the arrow to stop short of that kind of follow-up."

In spite of superficial differences, his fellow ministers, in almost every case, were happy to welcome him and cooperated with him. The audiences, too, were most receptive. To prepare for his meetings, Andrew usually sent ahead parcels of his latest books, usually twenty at a time, to serve as preparatory messages.

Random comments from letters by Andrew about a series of his meetings provide us with a little flavor of his activities:

"I arrived after a rattling drive of twenty hours. The spiritual shaking here has been very real, but at first we felt like we were speaking against a dead wall. We are expecting large blessings. . . .

Our services here are over, resulting in deep feeling among many, and open confession among some. We praise God. . . . I had hard work here, doing most of the talking, but the spiritual change in the people has so set me up that I hardly feel tired. God gives strength. . . . I feel one needs time to get more of God into one's life and work. Lord, teach us. . . . Such roads, truly like the Transvaal! This morning on awakening, for the first time I felt tired, but it is all right now. . . .

"Services began this afternoon in pouring rain. I am humbly asking the Father to command it to cease. . . . I have begun on the way to write a Dutch book on Hebrews, which I look to God to bless very much. . . . Testimonies here are in abundance and very clear, of blessings received by people who had long feared the Lord but had not known what salvation by faith was. And some twenty confessions of conversion. . . . Had some clear cases of entrance into light and joy, and in the next service a number of people came forward again. A young girls' prayer meeting has started, also a boys'. . . . Much proof of God's blessing on the services and so many testimonies to the effect: 'I thought I must be, or get, or do something. And now I see it was all wrong. I now trust the living Jesus.' The joy is great in many hearts. I meet a lot of people who are the fruit of former special serv-ices. . . . So the Lord proves the work is not in vain. To His name be the praise!"

As Andrew received warm hospitality wherever he went as an evangelist, he likewise extended a generous welcome to other evangelists who visited South Africa. Only a few might be mentioned: John R. Mott, F. B. Meyer, Spencer Walton, John McNeil, Mark Guy Pearse, Gipsy Smith, and Donald Fraser.

Dr. F. B. Meyer wrote of the courtesies shown him in South Africa which he recognized would not have been given him if Andrew had not come to welcome him upon arrival and attend his meetings even when he was in his eighties. "It was of untold help that my earliest meetings should receive the endorsement and blessing of the recognized father and leader of the Dutch Church."

In spite of his advanced years, Andrew was always open to new means of sharing God's Word with the people. His interest was awakened upon hearing about "One-day Conferences" (two or three sessions in a particular church but lasting a single day). This appealed to the limited strength of Andrew and he wrote a leaflet promoting the scheme, which was taken up by many churches. Subjects were suggested which would be of spiritual benefit to the congregation and would enable the minister to know the needs and attitudes of his people better. When Andrew participated in them, though he was frail and thin, it was reported that he seemed, each time he ministered, to overcome his weakness and amazed all with his fire and energy.

In 1904 Andrew founded the Prayer Union, which was open to Christians who had pledged themselves to devote at least a quarter of an hour daily to praying for others and also for the furtherance of the Kingdom of Christ throughout the world. When Andrew died, the name of the Union was changed to "The Andrew Murray Prayer Union" to serve as a lasting memorial to his influence as a man of prayer and his sincere pleas regarding the role and the power of prayer in the council of God. In later years, this Union incorporated the Revival Union and the Abundant Life Movement.

In his closing years, Andrew was described as "of medium height with spare frame, thin grey beard, hair that hung in great locks about his neck, and deep, mystic, hazel eyes." Until that accident in Natal which permanently injured his spine, his bearing was upright, his step rapid, and his frame so wiry that it could endure the greatest strain which circumstances or hard work could impose. That injury changed his figure into one which was stooped and had an almost deformed appearance. He eventually resorted to sitting on a high stool while preaching, though this did not in the least affect his sincere and passionate delivery.

Even in old age, Andrew's voice was full and resonant, and there was something peculiarly sincere and engaging in the heartiness of his greeting to all. He possessed an exceptionally keen memory not merely for facts set down in books, but for matters which he had observed or which had been told him in years gone by. He was careful in attending to details, regular in hours of his daily schedule, in answering his correspondence, punctual in keeping appointments and settling accounts.

The ultra-sternness of the early days of his ministry evolved into a gentle, open, loving quality that tempered all his relations with people. He maintained a strong sense of humor, though he kept it under restraint because of his official, public positions. It would break out at unexpected moments, however. Often it saved the day during tense times when he was moderator of the synod, and it relieved and calmed an excited assembly.

Andrew had a ready gift for having just the right illustration or anecdote at appropriate moments. As an example, after holding a series of gospel meetings at a village in the Free State, Andrew announced a "testimony meeting" before the country people would disperse to their farms again. To get the meeting started, he put to them the startling question, "What is the first sign of a man's having taken too much wine?" After a pause, he answered his own question. "Talkativeness! And now," he continued, "what should be the first sign of a man's having received a blessing from God at this conference? Why, talkativeness—not a convivial but a spiritual talkativeness. For that is what the Apostle Paul says: 'Be not drunk with wine, but be filled with the Spirit, *speaking to one another*. . . .'"

During one of Andrew's evangelistic conferences in Natal, a certain speaker protested against the extravagant language and expressions of joy, praise, and elation used by some of the people who attended Holiness meetings.

Andrew replied tactfully, "Yes, some sincere and godly people, in the overflowing fullness of their experience of a new truth, may not always express themselves conservatively, or perhaps in the accustomed manner. But we must not reject the experience because of expressions which may accompany it. That reminds me of the old days when we used to travel by ox-wagon. At the end of the day's journey, the first thing we did was light the fire, boil the water, and put in the meat. While we watched the cooking process, we saw the scum rise to the surface. Of course we skimmed it off and threw it away, but we did not throw away the meat!"

Naturally there were some who criticized Andrew's messages, but he always took care not to defend himself. Sometimes, of course, there were false reports that others wished to correct on his behalf out of their love and loyalty. On one such occasion, a close friend resented very strongly some damaging criticisms concerning a published address of Andrew's. On his own, the friend prepared a vindication which he read to Andrew and asked his advice about publishing it.

"Do you think this reply will convince our critic?" Andrew asked.

"No, I don't suppose it will."

"Then what will be the use of publishing it? It will only lead to further controversy from which nothing will be gained." The matter was dropped and left to the Lord.

His versatile interests were seen in the widely varied aspects of life on which he touched: total abstinence, unity among Christians, faith healing, and the Afrikaaner interests. These may seem to the average person matters so diverse that only a miracle could join them. To Andrew it was nothing out of the ordinary to move from one to the other subject with the greatest of ease.

Andrew had no problem with integrating spiritual life and matters of the real world about him. They were all one to him. A certain Christian gentleman approached Andrew to discuss a business problem but hesitated because Andrew had, just a few minutes before, finished delivering a most spiritual message to a congregation. Andrew was so keenly attentive to the business immediately that the man was quite amazed.

"How can you manage, sir," he asked, "to turn with such ease from spiritual exhortation to practical business detail?"

"Why," said Andrew, "surely *this* is the Master's business as well as the other."

25

The Family Touch

The most familiar title for this servant of God was "Andrew Murray of Wellington." Andrew spent forty-six years of his ministry in that city as his home base, living in two different homes: in the parsonage near the church for twenty-one years until he passed it over to his associate pastor in 1892, then in his personally built residence Clairvaux, on a portion of ground belonging to the Training Institute. The latter home was surrounded by buildings of the Institute at rather close quarters. But since it was on a little ridge, the view of valley, gardens, vineyards, waving cornfields and Dutch homesteads, all fading away to the distant, lofty Drakenstein Mountains, justified its location.

It was on the broad, stone veranda on the sunny north of the house that Andrew wrote his books, received his visitors, and transacted business when the weather was favorable. He never wearied of gazing at the quiet pastoral scene, remote from the dusty highways of life and throb of the restless world.

All his life Andrew appreciated beauty, delighting in the sights and smells of gardens, particularly roses, which held for him memories of gardening by Emma and himself no matter where they were in the pastorate. Purple lilacs reminded him of Scotland and his boyhood.

When a vase full of violets was set on his study table, he would frequently lift it and draw a long whiff with evident enjoyment. The changing colors of nature caused him always to exclaim of the lavish goodness of God in making so much beauty for His creatures to enjoy.

We have met Emma throughout this story and came to know her as a true life-partner. She was an affectionate, understanding wife, faithful mother, spiritual counterpart, who was in closest sympathy with Andrew's work. With joy and enthusiasm she shared his heavy congregational labors.

For about fifty years of his life, one or more young people, chiefly boys, lived in the Murray parsonage, unofficially "adopted" as part of their family, educated in the hope of supplying the need for Christian workers. It was wonderful to see how Emma opened her heart to these "extra children." In letters to her family one can hardly distinguish between her interest in the formation of the character of her own children and those living in their household.

Although their own family was so large that it might have fully occupied her, being a woman of culture and learning, she was involved in many of the educational and training ventures which Andrew established through the years. In the early days at Bloemfontein she shouldered the care of the students at Grey College in connection with Andrew's rectorship. During the revival of 1860, she started a ladies' prayer meeting at Worcester which continued as a spiritual force through many years. At Worcester and Cape Town she pioneered in enlisting children for work-circles for the missionary cause and worked untiringly in the Sunday Schools. As her children grew up, she became more free and was able to do even more.

Emma was intensely interested in the ministry of the Huguenot Seminary, the Missionary Training Institute, and Friedenheim, a successful training school for women workers. She helped start a successful industrial school for poor white girls, and she was president from the beginning of the Women's Missionary Union, whose marvelous growth and wide influence were due largely to her unceasing labors and wise counsel.

Emma's disposition was such that a young seminarian who lived in their home for an extended period complimented her, "She was such a gracious, wifely, motherly person that *not* to be in harmony with her would be self-condemnation."

As Andrew and Emma advanced in years they also grew wiser, but in many ways they kept an almost youthful enthusiasm for new ideas and interests beyond those of their immediate surroundings. Emma's faith in her husband and his multiple ministries for the Lord was known to all. Andrew could always count on his wife's alert, intelligent response to any of his new schemes and on her help and energy in carrying them out. Many acknowledged that without Emma to spur him on and to take other pressures away from him, it is doubtful Andrew could have produced the enormous output of religious writings in his busiest years.

When the Murrays moved to Wellington they had nine children. The two youngest died the following year, but in 1873 another son, the last of the family, was born. Most of the child training fell to Emma since Andrew was away on evangelistic missions much of the time. She did an exemplary job and drew to herself the lasting love and appreciation of her children.

Eight children, four sons and four daughters, lived to adulthood. Their eldest son, Howson Rutherfoord, was the first of these to die, at the young age of twenty-three. Not being a strong lad, he had been unable to continue higher studies so entered business with his uncle in Cape Town. There he died unexpectedly while his parents were absent on ministry in the Transvaal.

Their eldest daughter, Emmie, joined the Salvation Army, reaching the rank of staff-captain and serving until she resigned to become director of a Christian institution for the rescue of young girls and unfortunate women. Mary, the second daughter, became a missionary among African tribes. The third daughter, Catherine Margaret (Kitty), pursued an educational career and occupied important positions in schools, first as principal of the branch Huguenot Seminary at Bethlehem and later at Graaff-Reinet. The youngest daughter, Annie, was Andrew's faithful and zealous private secretary and traveling companion during his last twenty years.

John and Charles became missionaries among the tribes, Charles taking a pastorate after his wife died in the malarial climate of

Nyasaland. In his later years he again became a missionary at Mochudi. The second eldest son, Andrew Haldane, was a most gifted and intellectual lad, having studied at Cambridge and returned to the Cape to pass his examination for the degree of M.A. He became a most diligent director of schools until he changed his occupation to engage in farming at Graaff-Reinet. A highly respected member of the community, he became a representative in the House of Assembly. When World War I broke out, he volunteered as a private for the East African campaign and was promoted to lieutenant. Unfortunately, he was killed in action in 1916 at the age of fifty in an attempt to save the life of a wounded fellow-countryman. He left behind a wife and three children.

Through Andrew's initiative, it became a habit among the scattered family members to pray especially for each other every Sunday evening and sing the hymn that was associated with the elder Murray's departure from Scotland: "O God of Bethel, by whose hand Thy people still are fed." Family reunions of the many scattered Murray families in South Africa, descendants of Andrew Murray, Sr., were held a number of times.

In 1906 one reunion was recorded at which sixty-eight descendants were present. Andrew himself was there, and Emma was keenly missed, having died the year before. Andrew refreshed the memories of the younger generation about the pioneer days of his father. "Our father came to this country a solitary man, and God has made of him a great host."

A significant cause to praise God was "that of all of Papa Murray's grandchildren, there was *not one* of whom we had cause to be ashamed." Special prayer was offered for the fourth generation that they, too, might choose the God of their fathers as their God. "You will not play football less successfully for choosing to serve God," they were reminded.

A nephew, Andrew Charles Murray, cautioned the group that privileges bring obligations. "We are very highly privileged in being heirs to the prayers of our parents, grandparents and great-grandparents, but we should in turn pray for *our* children. They may change their names by marriage or go to the ends of the earth, but they cannot escape the mark placed upon them, for in their veins flows the blood of generations of praying ancestors."

One of the reunions was held on August 25, 1950, when eighty-six mainly direct descendants met in Andrew Murray Hall in Stellenbosch. Among them were a number of octogenarians who remembered "the early days." On that occasion many of the third, fourth, and fifth generation met one another, some for the first time. A moving account of this gathering ended with the report that they were all led in a simple prayer of rededication, in the hope that they, too, might do their utmost to follow in the footsteps of their forefathers to bring glory to the Kingdom of God and honor to His name.

Many men have one face toward the outside world and another toward their family and home. They can be merry and agreeable enough with strangers, but at home it is a different matter. One of the young men who was studying for the ministry stayed with the Murrays for an extended time and observed the following about Andrew:

"He was a highly strung man. His preaching was so enthusiastic, his gestures so unrestrained that he was wearing himself out. The doctor ordered him to sit while preaching. Such an output of nervous energy might well mean some reaction at home, some irritation with his wife, some unevenness in his dealings with his children, some caprice with the stranger within his gates. *But no!* I never knew him thrown off balance.... He was solid gold throughout."

One of his biographers, W. M. Douglas, testified that he wrote as one who "had ample opportunity to judge" Andrew's temperament because he worked in a mission organization with him. At different times he was both Andrew's guest and host, a fellow traveler to conventions, and with him in committee meetings and under trying circumstances. He bore tribute, "I have never seen the slightest impatience, irritability or anger in him. To me he seemed the loveliest and humblest of men, the embodiment of holiness as well as its exponent. I admired his consistency and exalted spirituality. My own ministry was transformed largely by his books thirty-five years ago in England."

Andrew practiced what he preached, particularly regarding prayer. A friend recalled what a perfectly natural way he brought everything to the Lord in prayer. One day at the Murray table there was a guest who was assisting with special evangelistic services. He was argumentative and rather bent on having his own way in a certain matter. It was being discussed at dinner. . . . Suddenly Andrew announced, "Let us ask God!" Immediately everyone knelt at the table while Andrew prayed. Apparently the man became rather embarrassed about his attitude and when everyone rose, he was silent and did not pursue the argument. Andrew had a wonderful tenderness and skill in dealing wisely even with overbearing people.

Andrew's daughter, Emmie, recalled that in the earlier days of her father's ministry, although he romped happily with them at play, yet the children tended also to fear him because he was so stern. But after his time of enforced silence due to the throat problem and his healing, his relationship with everyone seemed to change remarkably, almost to reflect a different personality. "At that time God came so near to father. He saw even more clearly the meaning of a life of full surrender and simple faith. He began to show in all relationships that constant tenderness, unruffled lovingkindness, and unselfish thought for others which increasingly characterized his life thereafter. At the same time, father lost nothing of his strength or determination."

Three grandsons, the children of his son John, spent ten years of their lives at Clairvaux for their education. Andrew's family never regarded him as a plaster saint upon a pedestal, but a warm and understanding person, totally approachable, whom they dearly loved and from whom they could learn much about nearly everything. Andrew's grandchildren and the children of nephews and nieces always enjoyed a welcome at the home of Grandpa or "Oupa" as they addressed him in Dutch. He spent much time chatting with them on their level, holding the young ones on his lap, reading to them, and letting them romp with his stout ebony walking stick for a hobby horse.

Andrew walked with God, but he also walked joyfully among his family and his fellow men.

26

Not Sunset, But Promotion

A friend recalled that Andrew's energy and strength for work was something unusual, even with advancing age and intensive travel. One day after a prolonged trip together, Emma said to her husband, "My dear, I think we ought to go home now. After all, we are getting old."

He replied, "Speak for yourself only, Mother. I don't want to die yet. There is still too much to be done."

At a certain public meeting where people were present who did not ordinarily go to religious meetings, a lady who had never seen Andrew watched him ascend the pulpit steps, frail and grey and stooped.

"Who is that old man?" she asked. "What a shame to make him go up those steps to preach!"

A friend of Andrew's sitting next to her thought to himself, *My dear lady, do you have a surprise coming tonight!*

As Andrew got up to speak he seemed to grow tall and majestic, and he spoke loudly and forcefully on behalf of a new mission work opening up in the Sudan. "Forward!" was his cry. So surprised was the lady that her pity gave way to reverence.

"What a voice for such a body!" she exclaimed. Clear as a bell, with irresistible power and command, Andrew proclaimed God's words in tones which knew no hesitation or defeat.

People in Europe and America were as impressed by Andrew's quiet humility and manner when he met and conversed with them as they were enthralled by his impassioned utterances. He did have severe critics, but even they admired his Christlike bearing as he heard and replied gently to their objections. It was written of him: "As the tree that bears the most fruit bends lowest and almost breaks under its own weight, so the holier he grew in advancing years and the more famous he became, the humbler he appeared, and the more his very face shone with the glory within."

Another student who lived with the Murrays commented, "There was no mid-autumn spoiling of the crop, but the whole matured harvest was fully gathered in without shortcoming and without loss—and what a harvest!"

"I saw him five months before his death, and his venerable face shone like Alpine mountains with the glow of the setting sun, so radiant, so gracious with the purity within," wrote a friend.

On his last birthday he was asked whether he felt any disappointment that God allowed his lameness and deafness to keep him from a more active life.

"Oh no, it is a kindly dispensation of my Father's providence," he replied contentedly. "God has shut me out from the life of ceaseless activity which I led in former years, and shut me in to greater quiet in which I can give more time to meditation and prayer. In the solitude and silence the Lord speaks precious messages to me which I try to pass on to others through my writing."

His exhortation to others on his last birthday was, in the spirit of the aged disciple John writing in his first epistle, "Children of God, let your Father lead you. Think not of what you can do, but of what God can do in you and through you."

"What are you doing sitting so quietly in the sun, Father?" his daughter once inquired.

"I am asking God to show me the need of the Church and to give me a message to meet the need. Children, remember to bask in the love of God as we bask in the sunshine of a winter's day."

There was no generation gap between Andrew and young people, even in his final years. All the societies that worked among the youth had a special place in his heart, and he gave them his full support. He prayed and yearned to lead young people to a full surrender of their lives and their energy to the Lord Jesus Christ. The Christian Endeavor movement was one of his keenest interests. He became and remained president of the society in Wellington for the remainder of his life. Both English and Dutch branches were established in South Africa. It was to this organization that Andrew dedicated his book *The Mystery of the True Vine*.

The Students' Christian Association was another of Andrew's concerns. This group united with two others and formed the nucleus of the Volunteer Movement for those who felt the call of the Lord to missionary work. His joy was great when his youngest son and two nephews joined this group and went to Nyasaland.

Andrew so loved the young people that he always invited them in for a quiet talk, resulting in life-changing influences upon them. One of the younger members of his family remarked about the aged Andrew, "Uncle Andrew never grows old." He was the embodiment of the description of the Psalmist, "He will still yield fruit in old age and shall be full of sap and very green" (92:14).

In Andrew's eightieth year, as a result of the establishment of the Laymen's Missionary Union, a missionary crusade was inaugurated with the weight of the responsibility and work falling upon him. He traveled far and wide through the country giving rousing addresses on behalf of missions. People were amazed how he, such an old man, could stand it.

One of his daughters warned, "Father, you will die on the train during your strenuous travels!"

"No, my child," he answered, "I shall not. I shall die in my bed." And this proved to be true.

The last few years before his death he took a long tour of up to five weeks once a year, and shorter journeys between, giving many addresses along the way to churches, conventions, mission groups, ministers' meetings, and congresses. At one point his daughter records that he preached twenty-eight times in twelve days, and it was *energetic preaching*! Afterward, from a full heart he would pour out praise and thanksgiving for traveling mercies, and intercessions on behalf of the work and for the friends whom he met on the tours. One of his ministerial brethren remarked, "He never repeats himself." One secret of his power was that every message was freshly received for the occasion. He did not offer stale bread to hungry souls.

At home between tours he did not collapse or take a well-earned rest. He was just as energetic as when in public. He usually dictated letters and books both in the morning and afternoon, but was always ready to meet friends who came to see him, never considering them interruptions. He would always pray with them on the broad veranda in front of his study which was his favorite place to sit quietly, pray and meditate when not writing.

World War I caused Andrew much sorrow, both for the turmoil of the nations and for his loved ones who were involved. He was interested in the war news day by day and took many illustrations from it for his messages. He was excited to learn about the development of new technologies like submarines, machine guns, and "fights in air ships."

Commenting on his manner during old age, a member of his family wrote, "Father speaks very quietly now with very little exertion but with great spiritual power. His seems like a voice on the verge of eternity, of one just ready to go on living while God wills. He is glad to live to deliver God's messages, but he talks little and conserves all his strength for work. Yet he has never been more bright and joyous in his whole life, so restful and peaceful. The world and all its interests seem in abeyance, and God's Kingdom and its concerns absorb his thoughts and heart. He has never lost touch with the life that is around him."

Andrew had been suffering from hardening of the arteries for some years, and late in 1916 suffered an attack of influenza which left him very weak. One of his biographers describes it as "God gently taking down the pins of the earthly tabernacle."

It was during his slow recovery that the news came of the tragic death of his second son in action on the battlefield. For some weeks the family kept the news from him because of his physical weakness, but when he was informed, he bore his deep sorrow with Christian courage.

During his recovery, he could be found bundled in a wrap and sitting in the sun on the veranda of his shore cottage at Kalk Bay looking out over the sea.

"Just look at the sea—what beautiful waves! How full the sea appears to be today, just like the love of God, so boundless, so vast, so free, so full. Can we look upon this beautiful ocean and doubt the love of God? Does not each wave seem to say to us, 'Have faith in God? He is so wonderful, so mighty. He is the Almighty.'

"Annie—where is Annie? I want to write so that all may know about this wonderful, mighty God, so loving, so tender, so unutterably worthy to be trusted and believed in by perishing mortals who are so unable to grasp His greatness and majesty and might."

During the nights when he could not sleep, he poured out his heart in prayer for ministers, for God's people, and for his country. "Pray, pray, pray for the nation that it might be a righteous nation," he would often plead.

His mind was always on the next book he wanted to write. When a friend wrote about his little child dying, the word "promotion" was used. Andrew's fertile mind was sparked: "The word 'promotion' has given me a thought for a new book. *Promotion is the favor of God.* I will write very simply how we may obtain it, so that the most ignorant can understand. First I will write about the favor of our great God; second, that we obtain it only through Christ; and lastly, that it is applied by the Holy Spirit."

Like the aged apostle John in his writings, so Andrew's thoughts centered on the *love of God* as he prepared to embark on the next stage of his eternal life. Just before his death he said, "The great and wonderful God wants to live out His life in us. He can do so only as we *dwell in love*. We can dwell in love only as Christ lives out His life in us, when we are fully yielded to Him. Let us then surrender ourselves to Him so that more of God's great and wonderful life may be lived in us."

On the last evening of his life as he was preparing for bed, he said, "We have such a great and glorious God that we ought to be always rejoicing in Him." Then he prayed, "Oh, ever-blessed and glorious God, satisfy us with Thy mercy that we may rejoice and be glad in

Thee all our days. Satisfy me that I may rejoice and be glad *always* in Thee." He literally died in communion with his Heavenly Father.

His final words were to his daughter. "Have faith in God, my child. Do not doubt Him," and "God is worthy of trust." On the eighteenth of January, 1917, at the age of eighty-eight, Andrew Murray peacefully met his beloved Lord face to face.

On the day of his funeral, shops and places of business were closed and all Wellington assembled in church to testify of their love and respect for the man of God who was known in so many of the churches of Christendom. His burial was in the churchyard near the Dutch Reformed Church, the site being immediately to the right of the main entrance. Telegrams poured in from the highest officials of the land and from the Church worldwide.

There were countless tributes to Andrew but only a few sentences will be selected to sum up his life: "Andrew Murray never sought fame. Apparently he was a man without ambition, except the ambition so characteristic of St. Paul, 'to preach the gospel' and 'to be well-pleasing to God.' In the days of his prime, his appeals stirred thousands, for his influence in the pulpit was magnetic. His tremendous earnestness swayed men's minds as the wind sways the cornfield. . . .

"He was essentially a man of prayer, and at the same time, a man of affairs. The eternal world was to him an intense reality, not a matter of speculation: things spiritual, in his case, dominated the temporal. To Andrew Murray, prayer meant unbroken communion with the Unseen and intercession for others, fellowship in feeling, and suffering with the Church of God in all portions of the globe. . . .

"Every new book he wrote was welcomed because it was fresh and stimulating. . . . Life for him meant simply that all activity was to be permeated and purified by the sense of the Eternal presence. . . . He was always pressing on—another mission given by God to perform, a message still to proclaim, a book or two still to be written. Some years ago a friend approached him with the request, 'Will you not give us some of your reminiscences?' The answer was characteristic: 'I have far better things to do than to talk and write about myself.' A mystic, a prophet, and a humble-minded follower of the Master, his has been a full life."

Because the passion of Andrew's life was to share with others through his writings that which he found to be most precious, people throughout the world have received fullness in Christ. Andrew Murray left a rich spiritual legacy of which we are joyful heirs!

— — — — —

Epilogue

The "Andrew Murray Family" in South Africa consists of all the descendants of the Rev. Andrew Murray, Sr., of Graaff-Reinet, who came to South Africa from Scotland in 1822. He married Maria Stegmann of Cape Town in 1825.

The couple had sixteen children, of whom eleven reached adulthood. Of these, nine were married and had descendants. They are now referred to as the "Nine Branches of the Graaff-Reinet Murray Family Tree." All nine of the married children were ministers of the church (the five sons) or married to ministers of the church (the four daughters).

Some of these branches already number several hundred descendants, of which the majority still live today. The tendency that several, even a majority, of members of a household chose church and mission related careers, continued for generations in several branches and sub-branches of the family, even to this day. Many books, articles, newsletters, etc., have been written (and will probably still be written) about and by these family members, whose influence on mission work in Africa and on education, church affairs, and spirit-ual life in Southern Africa can be described as quite substantial.

Many, for example, chose medical or other careers in the mission fields. There surely are many unsung heroes among the missionary members of the family, as there always are among workers in mission fields all over the world! One can often see from their lives that mission work is both humbling and spiritually enriching in the extreme. But not all branches and sub-branches continued with the example of church-related careers. Many subbranches and individuals moved in other directions.

The Andrew branch, descendants of the second eldest son (Dr. Andrew Murray, Jr., of Wellington, the subject of this book, who married Emma Rutherfoord) is in numbers today the second smallest of the nine branches of the family. Of Andrew and Emma's eleven children, eight reached adulthood but only three married and had offspring. The two eldest children, Emma Maria Murray and Mary Ellen Murray, never married but became missionaries and reached the ages of eighty and seventy-eight respectively. The eldest son, Howson Rutherfoord Murray, died at age twenty-three. The second son, Andrew Haldane Murray, initially considered a theological career but, to his parents' deepest disappointment, decided against it and followed a teaching career before eventually changing to farming. Several of his descendants are still prominent and highly respected and loved members of the farming community of Graaff-Reinet and surrounding districts. His only surviving daughter, Emma Drake, settled and married in England and, in June 1998, reached the age of eighty-five. She became the last surviving grandchild of Andrew and Emma, after her last surviving cousin, Prof. Andrew Haldane Murray of Cape Town, passed away in 1998 in his ninety-fourth year.

The Graaff-Reinet Andrew Murray family of South Africa considers itself part of the worldwide Murray Clan. The first formal register published on the Graaff-Reinet Murrays was an addendum at the back of a book published in 1909 by Maria Neethling, eldest daughter of Andrew Sr. and sister of Andrew Jr. The title of the "private circulation only" book is *Unto Children's Children*. It relates short histories and sketches of the founding parents and of the first generations of the nine branches. It refers to the Family Covenant and to the family's hymn (See Chapter One of this book), and the purpose "to keep up the bond of union, so that our children's children may remember that they are all covenanted children."

Emma Horn, a member of the daughter Jemima branch, published a second family register in 1956, and Caroline Murray, a member of the Charles Murray branch, prepared a third register in 1978. Based mainly on many years of further work by Caroline and others, a proof edition of a fourth register was published in 1996 by *Koos Reyneke* (Jemima branch) and further work on it continues with family team effort. The register is now being kept on computer.

The first major family reunion was held in 1922 to commemorate the centenary of the arrival in South Africa of the "stamvader" (founding father) Andrew Sr. in 1822. The location was the original historic parsonage "Reinet House" and its surrounding buildings at Graaff-Reinet, where the Graaff-Reinet Museum is currently based. At that reunion, they took a group photo of all present on the front steps of Reinet House. A series of *Family Newsletters* followed for a number of years (at least seven or eight editions were published from September 1923 to December 1928).

The second major reunion was held at the same venue fifty years later in 1972 commemorating 150 years. This was followed by similar events in 1982, 160 years, and 1994, the 200th birthday of Andrew Sr. (See photo in this book, to our knowledge, the only photo ever taken of him.)

Not to glorify man but for the glory of God, the family decided at the 1972 meeting to maintain contact by way of a continuation committee through which various initiatives could be addressed, such as the establishment of a *Family Fund* mainly to support mission work.

Through the years, a number of missionary initiatives and other religious causes have been supported in this way in South Africa as well as in other African countries.

In one year, through a special effort, an urgently needed new vehicle was donated to the Students' Christian Movement of Malawi (SCOM), an organization which also received regular annual donations through the years. Specific initiatives in Soweto, the vast sub-economic township on the outskirts of Johannesburg, have also been receiving support over many years.

A fairly regularly published annual *Family Newsletter* was introduced in 1974 and this has been maintained for more than twenty years. The logistics of distributing the Newsletter resulted in the development and maintenance of a computerized database and address list of family members, currently approaching 1,000 addresses. Closely linked to this is the computerized maintenance of the family register, as well as the possibility of perhaps at some future date a family website on the Internet. Increasing numbers of the Graaff-Reinet Murray family descendants are spreading out across the world.

Family gatherings of a sub-regional nature have been held from time to time, notably in Pretoria during the late seventies and eighties. Other initiatives included a commemorative plaque, in 1975 at the Millhouse of Clatt in Aberdeenshire, Scotland, where Andrew Sr. was born; the restoration of family gravestones in the Graaff-Reinet cemetery in 1982; and the registration in 1985 of the Andrew Murray Family Association and its newly designed family crest.

In addition to these and other initiatives originating from within the family, opportunities have periodically arisen for participation in initiatives originating from outside the family. In this context, the family contributed to the establishment, some years ago, of an annual *Andrew Murray Prize* for defined categories of locally published religious books in South Africa.

Many smaller family reunions have been and are being held from time to time, mostly by branches or sub-branches of the family and/or in connection with some special event. One example of the latter is the special family get-together held in Wellington on the fourteenth of May 1978 (Pentecost Sunday), after the nationally broadcast church service to commemorate the 150th anniversary of the birth of Dr. Andrew Murray.

As indicated before, the tendency is still encountered in a number of sub-branches of the family that several members of a household are very actively and even on a full-time basis involved in church activities of one or more denominations.

There is also a growing awareness in the family that many sub-branches and individual members are making their mark in totally different professions and spheres of society. These include politics, education, agriculture, sports, the arts, science and technology, the legal professions, and the economic field, to mention but a few.

Many examples can be cited of both the older and younger generations making their mark inside and outside the sphere of church and religion. This should clearly not be linked to family heritage or tradition.

The view of the younger generation today is increasingly that what is of importance is not so much to look back and appreciate and honor the memory, traditions and heritage of one's ancestry. Rather, it is important to address oneself towards the future and its opportunities with one's own convictions and, only as background and as and when considered appropriate, also through the spirit of "our children and children's children."

In this spirit, at the 1994 family reunion at Graaff-Reinet, the focus was shifted to some extent from the older generation to the younger generation. A workshop exercise drew attention to the role that especially the younger generation has to play in an ever faster changing world, country and society.

Only time will tell to what extent the family bonds and heritage might be able to make a constructive contribution in this context. We trust the Lord for that.

Teo Louw
Treasurer of the Andrew Murray Family Association
A Murray descendant in Pretoria

The Register of the Children and Grandchildren of Andrew Murray Jr. and his wife Emma

Andrew Murray, born May 9, 1828, in 1856 married Emma Rutherfoord who was born July 10, 1835.

As published in 1909 in the family "for private circulation only" book, *Unto Children's Children*.

(This has since been considerably adjusted, expanded and updated in various subsequent family registers prepared and published by members of the Andrew Murray family in South Africa, as indicated in the Epilogue. Up to 1998, the direct descendants of Andrew Jr. and Emma number slightly more than one hundred.)

Emma Maria, April 20, 1857
Mary Ellen, December 14, 1858
Catherine Margaret, August 12, 1860
Howson Rutherfoord, March 14, 1862
Annie Jemima, October 25, 1863
Isabella, May 31, 1865
Andrew Haldane, November 10, 1866
(Married Minnie Parkes, April 1897)
   Andrèe, March 9, 1898
   Kathleen Emma, June 18, 1902
   Robert, February 7, 1904

John Neethling, November 7, 1868
(Married Salomina Hansmeyer, 1895)
    Andrew Rutherford, October 1896
    Paul Milne, April 20, 1898
    Louis Botha, January 22, 1900
    Susan Elizabeth, February 17, 1904
Frances Helen, March 30, 1870
William Stegman, August 23, 1871
Charles Hugo, November 16, 1873
(Married Christina de Vos, January 26, 1904)
    Andrew Howson, April 21, 1905

Two Contemporary Testimonies from South Africa

I was born in South Africa, served in the South African Air Force during World War II, and was converted while employed as an aeronautical engineer with the Central African Airways in Zimbabwe. I answered God's call to full-time service in the pastorate of the Lutheran Church, from which I am now retired.

Several years ago I became passionately interested in Andrew Murray, his theology and his exploits for God. In my D.Th. thesis at the University of Stellenbosch, Murray plays a major role. I researched every possible reference work on him, both by his biographers and his critics. I was impressed by Leona Choy's extensive research into sources relevant to the Murray milieu and quote her at several points. The biography of Murray she wrote has been and still is a blessing to many.

I live not far from Montagu where the 1860 revival began before it spread to Worcester and beyond. I am even nearer to Wellington where Murray spent so much of his life, and where the institutions he established still stand as monuments to his accomplishments through God's enabling.

An amazing servant of God, he was unlike any other. He was known for living what he proclaimed: Christlikeness. Even to walk among those buildings in Wellington is to experience the melting presence of the God who sent spiritual revival in fulfillment of Joel 2:28, simultaneously in the United States and South Africa—so far apart geographically, yet both so dear to the heart of God. Whenever I read of the account of that revival, with tears I pray, "Oh God, won't you do it again?"

I am astounded at the continued interest shown in the writings of Andrew Murray who died so long ago (early in this century). His books are still being read and reprinted for new generations of readers worldwide. With many others, I enthusiastically welcome this new edition of Murray's biography by Leona, including fresh insights on the importance of his wife, Emma, to his life, ministry and writing.

Albert Brandt
Stellenbosch, 1998

I lived in Wellington for more than fifty years before I gained in-depth insight into the character of Andrew Murray, minister of the Dutch Reformed Church of Wellington during the past century. He was inseparably linked to the history of Wellington.

It happened that a friend gave me the book *Andrew Murray: Apostle of Abiding Love*, written by Leona Choy, an American author who was unknown to me. It was translated into Afrikaans as *Andrew Murray, Beelddraer van Ewige Liefde*. Before that, Andrew Murray was only a "distant saint" to me. This human and immensely readable story, however, changed that preconceived idea. It made me realize that the main character was, albeit highly gifted, still human, and that God works through ordinary people.

I first read this book many years ago, but its message has remained with me all these years, and I return to it ever so often. Leona Choy has now done additional research and updated this fascinating story of Andrew Murray, his writings—especially his personal and family life—and his tremendous and ongoing influence on Christians across the globe. Like many other lovers and readers of Andrew Murray, I look forward with great anticipation to the new revised edition of this book.

Winnie Rust
Wellington, 1998

Appendix of Murray Books

Some of Andrew Murray's major books currently in print in English are listed in alphabetical order by title. Synopses, dates, and background of their writing are included where available. Cross references to chapters in this book provide additional background.

Many of Murray's books were not written from start to finish as intended books. Some were reprints of articles he wrote for the official magazine of the Dutch Reformed Church of South Africa—first known as *De Gereformeerde Kerkbode* (1849 to 1879)— then called *De Christen* (1879 to 1883), and later named *De Kerkbode* (1884 to 1933). Others were compilations by Murray or others of his messages given in public on certain themes.

Chapter 23 of this book is a discussion of Andrew Murray's creativeness, writing habits, techniques, and the effect of his publications on the Christian world of his day. In various other chapters reference is made to events in his writing career.

Murray's most fruitful year of writing was 1895 when no fewer than sixteen of his publications appeared. Though seven were only short addresses of fewer than ten pages each, nine were substantial books averaging 135 pages. He was fond of the format of thirty-one or fifty-two chapters which could be read daily for a month or weekly for a year. In the last five years of his life he was particularly inclined to a "pocket size" series.

Abide in Christ

Written in 1864, this was one of Murray's earliest works. Subtitled "Thoughts on the Blessed Life of Fellowship with the Son of God," it was written in the old Dutch parsonage at Worcester as a manual to guide the many converts from the great revival of 1860. Within four years, more than 40,000 copies were sold. Eighteen years later Murray issued it as the first of his English books. The teachings were designed to prevent the all-too-frequent falling short of the glorious life of full salvation after the new birth. The format is daily meditations for one month on the depths of what Jesus meant in John 15:4 concerning abiding. He emphasized that it is most certainly within the reach of every new believer. (See Chapters 10, 11, 17, and 19 for background.)

Absolute Surrender

Published originally in 1895, these nine chapters are an exposition of what the author believed was the one great need of the Church and each believer. He summarized: "Your God in Heaven answers the prayers which you have offered for blessing on yourselves and for blessing on those around you by this one demand: Are you willing to surrender yourself absolutely into His hands?" (See Chapters 10 and 11.)

Abide in Devotion

First published in 1909, subtitled "Thoughts on the Holy Spirit in the Epistle to the Ephesians," this was originally a series of articles under that title written as helps for the quiet hour and printed in the *Lovedale Christian Express*. The purpose is that the believer might "realize what the standard of the true Christian life is as it is set before us in Ephesians, and what absolute, divine assurance it gives us that God is able and willing to make all that it contains true in our experience."

Be Perfect

Published originally in 1893, it was begun at the Murrays' favorite vacation spot at Kalk Bay on the last day of their annual vacation one year. Everyone was involved with last-minute preparations for departure, and there was Andrew, oblivious to all the confusion, sitting contentedly at a window overlooking the sea, quietly thrilled with a fresh message from the Lord and a commission to deliver it in print. In thirty-one chapters the author traces the term "perfect" through the Scriptures, seeking to understand the correct meaning from the context. He concludes that there is a perfection of which Scripture speaks which is possible and attainable, in fact, is a command to be obeyed with one's whole heart. It is obtained only by yielding to the leading of the Holy Spirit so that God may accomplish that perfection in us.

The Blood of the Cross

This book contains the last ten discourses of Murray on this subject, the first ten of which are published in the book *The Power of the Blood of Jesus*. This subject first gripped his attention on a trip to Europe, and on his return to South Africa in 1883 he gave messages on The Blood during Passion Week to his congregation at Wellington. This is a brilliantly researched, spiritually moving study of the power of the blood of Christ, the deepest mystery of redemption. The author asserts that there can be no freedom of approach to God nor fellowship with Him apart from the truly vital and powerful experience of the efficacy of the blood of Christ. Murray skillfully leads the reader to a full awareness of what that blood actually signifies.

Confession and Forgiveness

Originally published in 1895 under the title *Have Mercy Upon Me*, this book examines Psalm 51 phrase by phrase, revealing the classically simple message of God's forgiveness. (See Chapter 12.)

Daily Thoughts on Holiness

Edited in 1977, it is a compilation by Frank Cumbers of devotional readings for every day of the year (actually dated). The excerpts are taken from twelve of Murray's best known books and each reading is annotated with the source and page number.

Day by Day with Andrew Murray

Originally published in 1899 as *The Andrew Murray Year Book*, it contains paragraph-length excerpts from twenty-six of his works, one for each day of the year. The theme which M. J. Shepperson, the compiler, selected to tie these thoughts together is "that our Lord Jesus is willing to be far more to us than we know. All that we have enjoyed of Him is only a beginning."

Divine Healing

First published in English in 1900, each of the thirty-one chapters is based on a scripture related to healing. Murray regarded this book as the testimony of his faith in divine healing. "I can no longer keep silence," he wrote, "that this truth is in perfect accord with Holy Scripture and essential for everyone who would see the Lord manifest His power and His glory in the midst of His children." (See Chapters 17 and 18.)

Freedom From a Self-Centered Life

Subtitled "Dying to Self," first published in 1898, these are selections from the writings of William Law which have been edited by Murray. It consists of four dialogues between various individuals, interspersed with Murray's insightful comments. The chief thought is how to live in Christ above the average state of failure in which most believers are found, which has its roots in the self-life. (See Chapter 23 for an evaluation of Law's theology; also see the Introduction of *Wholly for God*.)

The Full Blessing of Pentecost

Subtitled "The One Thing Needful," it was first published in 1907. The author's purpose was to urge believers to lay aside everything to obtain this experience of power. This book expresses his intense fervor of writing surpassing any of his other works. The simple but most serious message is that "men ought everywhere to seek with one accord and with their whole heart to be filled with the Spirit of God." Murray emphasized that the filling with the Holy Spirit is for every believer to live in entirely and unceasingly. "Without it neither a Christian nor a church can ever live or work as God desires; so few have it or even seek it; God is waiting to bestow it; our self-life and the world hinder it; we obtain it by yielding all of ourselves for this pearl of great price."

Applying it to missions, Murray writes with all the fiery energy of his lifelong conviction: "To know what Pentecost means, to have its faith and its spirit, is the only power to evangelize the world in this generation. The pentecostal commission can only be carried out by a pentecostal church in pentecostal power!" (See Chapters 19, 20 and 21.)

Helps to Intercession

Published originally in 1898 in London under the title *Pray Without Ceasing*, these thirty-one short meditations on scriptures relating to aspects of prayer help the reader to pinpoint his own special petitions. The format for each day's reading is divided into two parts, "What to Pray" and "How to Pray," with space for personal prayer requests and notes. (See Chapter 13.)

The Holiest of All

This is a devotional exposition of Hebrews in 130 chapters originally published in 1894. Topics cover: the Presence of God; the Sphere of Christ's Ministry; Heaven; and Our Life and Service on Earth. The author's purpose was to show "how the Holy Spirit reveals the way into the Holiest as opened by the blood of Christ and invites us by faith in Christ to have our life there. It is as we yield our hearts to the leading of the Spirit to know Christ and look at Him, and believe in what is revealed, that the Spirit can take possession of us."

Holy in Christ

Published originally in 1887, it is the result of careful theological study coupled with warm evangelistic fervor. Subtitled "Thoughts on the Calling of God's Children to be Holy as He is Holy," the book comprises thirty-one readings for a month. It explores the possibility of the believer living the reality of a seemingly impossible command and expectation of his Lord. The author traces through the Scriptures what God meant to convey by the term "holy" and its centrality in Jesus. Murray has carefully explained for us "the conviction that we must be holy, the knowledge of how we are to be holy, the joy that we may be holy, the faith that we can be holy." (See Chapters 19 and 20.)

How to Raise Your Children for Christ

Published in 1886, this book was one of Murray's earlier works, written first in Dutch and later in English under the title *What Manner of Child Shall This Be?* It is also known as *The Children for Christ*. Its fifty-two short chapters deal with almost every aspect of child-raising. At Bloemfontein and later at Worcester Murray began the custom of monthly baptismal services when he would preach directly to the parents on this subject.

Concerning his philosophy of training children in the Christian faith, he wrote, "Surely it is obtainable, that instead of parental piety being diluted in children—this is so often spoken of as what we must expect—each succeeding generation of a God-fearing family ought to rise higher and higher. . . . The faith and the simplicity required for training children would perhaps be better training for the ministry than much that we consider great." Besides dealing with the principles of training, Murray set forth examples from the Old and New

Testaments concerning children: bringing them to the Lord and helping them grow in faith. (See Chapters 4, 5 and 23.)

Humility

Twelve messages published first in 1895 direct our attention to the humility that becomes us as those who have been created by God and which is indispensable for the fullness of the Christian life. "Pride must die in you, or nothing of Heaven can live in you. Look not at pride only as an unbecoming attitude, nor at humility only as a decent virtue: for the one is death, and the other is life; the one is all Hell, the other is all Heaven. . . . It is only in the possession of God that I lose myself." (See Chapter 10.)

The Inner Chamber and the Inner Life

Published originally in 1905, this book emphasizes the daily need of retirement and quiet for secret communion with God. The neglect of this holy habit, Murray explains, is the "root disease" from which thousands of believers are suffering, which explains the feebleness of their Christian life. Most of the chapters were first published in *The South African Pioneer.*

Among the topics considered are: The true spirit of prayer; the devotional reading of God's Word; the fellowship with God for which these are meant and by which alone they bring a blessing; the spiritual life which they are meant to strengthen and fit for daily duty in intercourse with the world; the service for the Kingdom of God in soul-winning and intercession. All of these truths, Murray claims, have their share in making our quiet time a source of joy and strength.

This is the only book Murray wrote on the "how to" of the devotional life. Most of his other books benefit us with the results of *his* quiet time before the Lord and *his* study of Scripture.

Jesus Christ: Prophet/Priest

Four addresses delivered by Murray at the Mildmay Conference at Barnet, near London, in 1895. Topics cover: Our Prophet, The Completion of the Priesthood, Our Way into the Holiest, and The Food of the Soul.

The Key to the Missionary Problem

(See Chapter 22 of this book for a complete background of its writing and its effect upon the Christians of Murray's day. Also Chapter 15.)

Let Us Draw Near

Published originally in 1894, these meditations on Hebrews 10:19–25 are twelve chapters from the larger book *The Holiest of All*, which is a comprehensive devotional exposition of the entire book of Hebrews. "This selected passage constitutes the very core of the Epistle, a summary of what had been taught in its first or doctrinal part, and indicates the chief thoughts which are to be enforced in the second half, the theme being: 'Let us draw near.' The state of those to whom Hebrews was written was just what we find in the churches of our day: a lack of steadfastness, of growth, and of power which arises from our not knowing Jesus aright."

Like Christ

This is a companion volume and sequel to *Abide in Christ* issued in English in 1884. Two years later 19,000 copies had been sold. Thirty-one daily meditations for a month draw a portrait of Christ "to show how, in the reality of His human life, we have an exact pattern of what the Father wants us to be. . . . This is no mere ideal of human imitation, but *through the power of the Holy Spirit* is a most blessed reality." Murray urges us to "gaze and gaze again, worship and adore, and the more we see Him as He is, the more like Him we must become . . . by letting the heavenly likeness reflect itself and shine out in our life among our fellow men. This is what we have been redeemed for, and let this be what we live for." (See Chapter 17.)

The Lord's Table

Published originally in 1897, it was written as a help to the right observance of the Holy Communion. Murray recommended concerning its study: "Christians, give yourselves, give your Lord, time to transfer His heavenly thoughts to your inner, spiritual life; meditate on the portion for the day and appropriate it, not just read it." The format is in three parts: Meditations for each day of the week before the celebration; Ten meditations on the details of the Sacrament for the morning of that Lord's Day; Meditations for each day of the week after the Communion. (See Chapter 13.)

The Master's Indwelling

Published originally in 1895, this book points out the difference between the life the average believer has been leading and the life that is abundantly available in the Spirit. It is designed to help the reader get out of the wilderness of defeat and into the Canaan of victory, with very practical instructions on how to make the change.

Money

First published in 1897 in London, this book offers Scriptural principles for stewardship of worldly possessions and counsel as to our attitude toward all things which are committed to us by God for His Kingdom.

The New Life

Published first in 1891, this book was written during Murray's travels between meetings. It is a brief manual on basic Christianity for new Christians. In a format of fifty-two chapters for a whole year's meditations, the six leading thoughts of the new life are dealt with: the Word of God; the Son, the gift of the Father; sin; faith; the Holy Spirit; and the holy life. Each chapter is amply fortified with Scripture references which the new convert is urged to diligently look up. Questions and comments on the text are included, and a related prayer to guide the new believer is part of each meditation.

The Power of the Blood of the Cross

On Murray's voyage to Europe in 1882 he meditated much on the expression "There is power in the blood" and recalled the popular hymn in which the words are repeated over and over. The more he meditated, the more he inquired, in the spirit of prayer: What is this power and why does it have such power? Upon his return the following year, he decided to give the answer to the question in a series of fifteen addresses delivered in his church during the season of preparation for Easter. Five more messages were subsequently added, and the whole was first published in a Christian magazine. Andrew maintained that the spiritual experiential power of the blood was absolutely necessary for the soul's conscious and joyous fellowship with God as well as for holiness.

For many years the first ten messages were published separately as *The Power of the Blood of Jesus* and the second ten as *The Blood of the Cross*.

The Pocket Companion Series

Because of the titles, this is often popularly called the "Secret Series." It consists of twelve short booklets of thirty-one meditations each, on Murray's most prominent themes: They are, in order of writing:

The Secret of Intercession
The Secret of Adoration
The Secret of the Faith Life
The Secret of Inspiration
The Secret of the Abiding Presence
The Secret of United Prayer
The Secret of Fellowship
The Secret of the Cross
The Secret of Brotherly Love
The Secret of Power from on High
The Secret of Christ Our Life
The Secret of the Throne of Grace (See Chapter 23.)

The Power of the Spirit

These are selections from the writings of William Law and edited by Andrew Murray. First published in 1896, this book is addressed first of all to clergy and those in positions of Christian leadership, "that they do not miss that which is the most essential part of their message and work—the power of the Spirit of God in and through us." Murray indicates in his extensive preface the differences between his evangelical position and Law's tenets, so that the reader may have spiritual discernment and at the same time benefit deeply from the insights of the writer. (See Chapter 23.)

The Prayer Life

Early in 1912 a ministerial conference was called at Stellenbosch and attended by about two hundred ministers, missionaries and theological students. The purpose was to explore the reasons for the low state of spiritual life which marked the Church—universal and local. Those who participated searched their hearts in God's presence and He spoke to many of them, resulting in confession, repentance and restoration. Murray spoke out strongly with his conviction that one of the deepest roots of the weakness of the Church and its leadership was the sin of prayerlessness. His messages on that subject were first published in Dutch, later in English, so that its central thrust—that in spiritual work *everything depends on prayer*—could reach a larger audience through the printed page. (See Chapter 13.)

The School of Obedience

Published originally in 1898, this book of eight chapters is dedicated to all Christian students. Among the chief topics that Murray sought to emphasize are that God asks, requires and expects the entire, day-by-day obedience of every believer; the enabling comes from the gift of His Son and the Holy Spirit; it is accomplished by absolute surrender to a life of abiding communion.

The Spirit of Christ

Published first in 1888, these thirty-one chapters for each day of the month comprise extensive studies from the Scripture on major aspects of the Holy Spirit and His indwelling in the believer and the Church. There are seventeen detailed and enriching notes constituting the last quarter of the book which deal in greater depth and doctrinal background with the topics set forth in the major part of the text. (See Chapters 10, 19 and 20.)

The Spiritual Life

Murray did not write this book in the sense of deliberately setting out to produce a publication. He came to America in the summer of 1895 and was invited to speak in many illustrious pulpits. So many had already been helped through his previous writings that, when he gave a series of lectures to the students at the Moody Bible Institute in Chicago, it was urged that the stenographic reports of those messages be compiled into a book. This was done with Murray's permission and revision, and this book is the result.

The State of the Church

This book was written in 1911 when Murray was eighty-three, in response to the Edinburgh World Missionary Conference. It was called "a book too faithful to be popular," and yet it became prominent because of its incisiveness in pointing out the lack of conversions, the striking decline of church membership, and the lack of spiritual vitality in the Church universal and local. Murray explained that he was not belittling the Church but sounding the trumpet call to seven times more prayer that the Church might be healed of its chronic spiritual weakness. He powerfully reiterated that "the Church of today [his day and ours] as a whole is suffering from the lack of one thing only—the heavenly enduement of power which made the whole apostolic Church triumphant—the pentecostal Spirit." (See Chapters 15 and 22.)

The True Vine

Sometimes titled *The Mystery of the True Vine*, it was published originally in 1897 in a format of thirty-one meditations on John 15:1–16, "as a help to young Christians to take up that position in which the Christian life must be a success." From the vineyards that surrounded the Murray home at Wellington, and from studying the principal livelihood of the farmers in his parish, he received inspiration for this book, which, with additional thoughts, were later collected into a larger volume entitled *The Fruit of the Vine*.

Murray kept an old vine stump upon his study table during the summer of 1897. We can imagine him meditating on its rough, brown, shapelessness day after day as he prayed and prepared messages for his people. This book was dedicated to young people, and specifically to the members of the Society for Christian Endeavor throughout the world. (See Chapters 13 and 26.)

The Two Covenants

Published first in 1898 and subtitled "The Second Blessing," these eighteen meditations attempt to show "what exactly the blessings are that God has covenanted to bestow on us; what the Covenant assures us will be fulfilled; what the hold on God Himself is which it thus gives us; and what the conditions are for the full and continual experience of its blessings." Six discourses are appended which deal with these topics: The Second Blessing; The Law Written in the Heart; George Müller and His Second Conversion; Canon Battersby; Nothing of Myself; and The Whole Heart.

Waiting on God

Murray prefaced the book in 1895 with the comments: "At all our conventions and assemblies too little time is given to waiting on God. Is He not willing to put things right in His own divine way? Has the life of God's people reached the utmost limit of what God is willing to do for them? Surely not. We want to wait on Him; to put away our experiences, however blessed they have been; our conceptions of truth, however sound and Scriptural; our plans, however needful and suitable they appear; and give God time and place to show us what *He* can do, what He *will* do. God has new developments and new resources. He can do new things, unheard-of things, hidden things. Let us enlarge our hearts and not limit Him." The book is arranged in thirty-one chapters for a month's readings. (See Chapters 14 and 21.)

Wholly for God

These 110 separate short selections from the writings of William Law were edited by Murray in 1893. They span the entire spectrum of the spiritual life and its development. "I know of no writer who equals Law in the clearness and the force with which the claims of God on man are asserted. God *is* all; God must *have* all; God alone must *work* all: around these central truths all his teaching gathers."

It was because the writings of Law in the early 1700s "were not at once easily apprehended," Murray explains, "that I have thought it to be of help to give such extracts from his books as would bring his more direct teachings on the spiritual life within the reach of all." Because some of Law's earlier works were controversial and theologically incomplete, it is essential for the reader to note carefully Murray's twenty-two page Introduction for proper discernment and appreciation of Law's writings. (See Chapter 23.)

With Christ in the School of Prayer

Sometimes titled *The School of Prayer*, it was published in 1885 subtitled "Thoughts on Our Training for the Ministry of Intercession." When the Dutch original was published, a fellow minister wrote, "Oh, why didn't the author give us this book twenty-five years ago? It is a perfect treasury. If Mr. Murray published nothing else, our country would owe him a great debt of gratitude." An outgrowth of a ministerial conference at George, Murray wrote it piecemeal traveling from town to town for special services. It includes an appendix on George Müller's life and the secret of his power in prayer.

Arranged in thirty-one chapters, the progressive teachings of Christ in regard to prayer are studied. The noted Dr. Alexander Whyte of Free St. George's gave a tribute to the influence of this book upon him: "Nothing I have read lately is half as good as *With Christ*. Your book goes to the joints and the marrow. You are a much honored man: how much, only the day will declare. Other books I have been reading are all able and good in their way, but they are spent on the surface of things. Happy man! You have been chosen and ordained of God to go to the heart of things. I have been sorely rebuked, but also much directed and encouraged by this book."

Working for God

This sequel to *Waiting on God* was first published in 1901, arranged in thirty-one brief chapters for a month's reading. The purpose is "to remind all Christian workers of the greatness and the glory of the work in which God gives us a share. As we see that it is God's own work that we have to work out, that He works it through us, that in our doing it His glory rests on us and we glorify Him, we shall count it our joy to give ourselves to live only and wholly for it."

The author indicated that, beside Christian workers, three more categories of believers can benefit from its contents: First, those who complain that they are apparently laboring in vain might find the cause of so much failure. "God's work must be done in God's way and in God's power of the Spirit." Second, it is also for another group who practically take no part in the service of the Lord. Murray's position is that "It is God's will that every believer, without exception, whatever his position in life, should give himself wholly to live and work for God." Third, it is also "for those who train others in Christian life and work, that they may find thoughts that will be of use to them in teaching the imperative duty, the urgent need, the divine blessedness of a life given to God's service." (See Chapter 15.)

─ ─ ─ ─ ─

Note: Some of Murray's books have been reprinted and reissued under different titles in recent years by various publishers. Some have been published in more contemporary language versions. (Contemporizations of Murray's books by Leona Choy are *The Key to the Missionary Problem*, *The Inner Chamber*, and *The State of the Church*.)

Bibliography and Resources

Documentation for certain basic facts of Andrew Murray's life comes from two out-of-print biographies listed below. Because the material even in those two volumes greatly overlaps, I decided it was neither possible nor advisable to interrupt the narrative by annotating sources within the text. I express my appreciation for these excellent books, whose publishers granted permission for use of the material.

The Life of Andrew Murray of South Africa, by J. Du Plessis. Marshall Brothers Limited, London-Edinburgh-New York, 1919.

Andrew Murray and His Message—One of God's Choice Saints, by Rev. W. M. Douglas. Oliphants Ltd., London-Edinburgh, 1926. Christian Literature Crusade edition, 1957.

Two sources for material dealing with the early life of Emma and the married life and family of the Murrays are books not available in North America, secured for me by friends in South Africa.

Young Mrs. Murray Goes to Bloemfontein (1856-1860), letters edited by Joyce Murray (The Murrays' granddaughter). A. A. Balkema, Cape Town, South Africa, 1954.

In Mid-Victorian Cape Town, Letters from Miss Rutherfoord, Edited by Joyce Murray. A.A. Balkema, Cape Town, South Africa, 1968.

Other useful sources were:

Unto Children's Children (published for private circulation within the Murray family in 1909). T. H. Hopkins and Son, Ltd., London. (Reprinted 1929 and 1987.)

The Joy of Service by Helen Murray (Andrew Murray's sister). Marshall, Morgan and Scott, Ltd., London and Edinburgh, 1935.

I also used information kindly supplied by Mrs. Raymond G. Slater (Charlotte Louise Murray), Andrew Murray's grandniece.
Certain other biographical material has been used, with permission, from:

The South African Dictionary of National Biography, Vol. I, Cape Town, South Africa.

The Encyclopedia of Southern Africa. National Boekhandel, Cape Town, South Africa.

Records of Murray family reunions, obtained from the South African Library at Cape Town and members of the Murray family.

Court records of the Judicial Committee during the civil suits involving the Dutch Reformed Church and Andrew Murray, published in 1867, located at the South African Library at Cape Town.

Various biographical materials (translated from the Dutch language) located at the University of South Africa at Cape Town.

I freely drew from the text of many of Andrew Murray's books for his teachings, for his imagined answers to questions I posed to him in the narrative, and for background material. In part, I used prefaces and introductions to his books currently in print for the synopses listed in the Appendix. I felt it would be burdensome and distracting to the reader to footnote or cross-reference these because some of the resources, even direct quotations, overlap.

In the Acknowledgments at the front of this book, I have recognized the help of living members of the Murray family in South Africa and other friends in that country to update and expand the present, new edition under a title different from my previous biography.

Leona Choy

Other Books by Leona Choy
Authored, edited or collaborated,
including foreign language editions

A Call to the Church from Wang Mingdao.
Andrew Murray: Apostle of Abiding Love.
    Spanish, Dutch, Chinese, Afrikaans, Korean editions.
    Revised as *Andrew and Emma Murray*. Currently published as this volume.
Are You Mad at Me, God? Jumping Illness Hurdles.
Celebrate This Moment! A Poetry Trilogy.
Christiana Tsai. Also Chinese edition.
Czeching My Roots: An Autobiograpny.
Hospital Gowns Don't Have Pockets! Why me? What now?
    Also Chinese edition.
How to Capture and Develop Ideas for Writing.
Let My People Go! Moses C. Chow with Leona Choy.
Living it UP! Meditations for Seasoned Saints.
My Dreams and Visions. Ted Choy with Leona Choy.
No Ground. Evelyn Carter Spencer with Leona Choy.
Powerlines. Also Chinese and Korean editions.
    Republished as *The Life-Changing Power of the Holy Spirit: Insights from Classic Christian Leaders.*
Release the Poet Within!
Singled Out for God's Assignment.
Touching China: Close Encounters of the Christian Kind.
The Widow's Might: Strength from the ROCK.
This Is Your Life: Write It!
Walk the Green Valley.

PUBLICATIONS
Fort Washington, PA 19034

This book is published by CLC Publications, an outreach of CLC Ministries International. The purpose of CLC is to make evangelical Christian literature available to all nations so that people may come to faith and maturity in the Lord Jesus Christ. We hope this book has been life changing and has enriched your walk with God through the work of the Holy Spirit. If you would like to know more about CLC, we invite you to visit our website:
www.clcusa.org

To know more about the remarkable story of the founding of CLC International we encourage you to read

LEAP OF FAITH

Norman Grubb
Paperback
Size 5¼ x 8, Pages 248
ISBN: 978-0-87508-650-7
ISBN (*e-book*): 978-1-61958-055-8